INTERVIEW AND INTERROGATION

ABOUT THE AUTHOR

Frank MacHovec is a licensed clinical psychologist who has been interviewing people for more than thirty years as an administrator, manager, therapist, teacher, a disabilities examiner and an expert witness in court cases ranging from child custody to murder. He has served on professional ethics committees in Virginia, Alaska and Canada and regularly speaks to state, national and international conferences on ethical and professional practice issues. In 1982 he was awarded a National Certificate of Recognition by the Psychologists in Public Service Division of the American Psychological Association. Presently, he chairs the Ethics and Legislation Committee of the Virginia Association for Marriage and Family Therapy and is a Vice President of that association.

Dr. MacHovec has authored more than fifty publications including articles in nine professional journals and books on expert witness testimony (1987), theories, history and applications of humor (1988), and the first book ever written on hypnosis complications (1986). He has taught at graduate and undergraduate levels and conducted workshops and in-service training for local, state, provincial and federal agencies, professional associations and private corporations in the United States and Canada.

He is a Fellow of the American Board of Medical Psychotherapists, an Approved Supervisor with the American Association for Marriage and Family Therapy, a Diplomate of the American Board of Psychological Hypnosis and a member of the Society for Personality Assessment, International Rorschach Society and the International Society of Hypnosis. He is listed in *Who's Who among Human Services Professionals, Who's Who in the South and Southwest* and in the international register *Men of Achievement.*

INTERVIEW
AND
INTERROGATION

A Scientific Approach

By

FRANK J. MACHOVEC, PH.D.

CHARLES C THOMAS • PUBLISHER
Springfield • Illinois • U.S.A.

Published and Distributed Throughout the World by

CHARLES C THOMAS • PUBLISHER
2600 South First Street
Springfield, Illinois 62794-9265

© *1989 by* CHARLES C THOMAS • PUBLISHER

ISBN 0-398-05578-5

Library of Congress Catalog Card Number: 89-4712

Printed in the United States of America
SC-R-3

Library of Congress Cataloging-in-Publication Data

MacHovec, Frank J.
   Interview and interrogation : a scientific approach / by Frank J.
MacHovec.
      p.   cm.
   Bibliography: p.
   Includes index.
   ISBN 0-398-05578-5
   1. Interviewing.   2. Questioning.   I. Title.
BF637.I5M33   1989
158'.3—dc19   89-4712
                                                              CIP

To the search for Truth:
    yours and mine,
    ours and theirs,
    past and present,
with many facets—
but one perfect jewel.

PREFACE

This book is for anyone who interviews or interrogates others. It applies to a variety of settings: job or school interviewing, legal practice, church work, medicine, mental health, security, news and investigative reporting, military debriefing and intelligence, law enforcement, sales and service industries. Obtaining information from others in today's world of multimedia information requires a thorough knowledge of human nature and sophisticated communications skills. Those are the two goals of this book.

The major emphasis is on **scientific** interview and interrogation based on the latest information on personality and behavior, emotion and motivation, needs and defenses, what is normal and what is abnormal. Chapter 1 introduces you to yourself, to your own unique personality and to the factors and forces that have made you who and what you are and that still influence you. Chapter 2 describes normal and abnormal behavior you can see in yourself but mostly in those you will be questioning. Chapter 3 describes how you and others interact, verbally by what is said, and nonverbally by what is done physically while saying it. Chapter 4 applies these learnings to the interview situation, and Chapter 5 does the same for interrogation. There are more than 40 exercises throughout the book to help apply what is learned.

Interviewing collects information, gets needed facts by question and close observation, then arrives at a conclusion. Interrogation does more, more intensively, and recreates an event or studies a subject in far more detail, its conclusion with far more serious consequences—prison or nationwide publicity and public reaction. Interviewing mines the raw material of questioning, and interrogation refines it into the hard steel of a finding, usually a confession, then conviction and sentencing in police work or nationwide media expose in investigative reporting. Interview and interrogation may both seem simple methods of searching for truth. After all, one person asks questions, the other answers. Not so! Both are quite complicated because they involve a complicated subject, the mind and behavior. To do them well requires specialized **scientific** techniques of close observation, strategic planning, and asking the right question in just the right way at the right time.

Interview and interrogation **are** specialized methods to study the many facets of truth—yours and mine, ours and theirs—in the past, and here and now. Good questioners "see with a third eye and hear with a third ear." In this way truth emerges of and by itself, through the fog of your own bias, assumptions and misperceptions, even through the fog in the minds of others. You are **half** of every interview and interrogation. If you do not see through your own "mental unfinished business" there may well be two people with impaired vision, the blind leading the blind. The best questioners are **scientific**—impersonal, objective, organized, meticulous—like the great artists and craftsmen of all ages.

This book is more comprehensive than others on the same subject. That may be an achievement and also a weakness. None of it has been written to impress you, but rather to provide you with the best information in a single volume to help you master the theory and practice of **scientific** interview and interrogation. It is hoped that you will find it a useful reference and refresher in the future. Though there was an effort to use clear, simple language, you may have to "reach up" to fully understand some of the material. Human nature is a fascinating study. May any extra effort be well worth it for you and give you a deeper, richer understanding of yourself and others. May it be for you as it was for Albert Einstein, who left his students with this parting thought: "Never lose a holy curiosity." That's good advice for scientists—and for scientific interviewers and interrogators.

Good luck!

Frank MacHovec

ACKNOWLEDGMENT

My grateful appreciation to Lieutenant Michael Jones of the Virginia Capitol Police, an experienced law enforcement officer, skilled interrogator, critic and colleague, for his suggestions to strengthen this book.

CONTENTS

INTERVIEW AND INTERROGATION

Chapter 1

YOU: WHO ARE YOU?

> I am always at a loss to know how
> much to believe of my own stories.
> Nathaniel Hawthorne
> (*Tales of a Traveler*, 1824)

If you could go on an unlimited totally financed worldwide vacation only once in your life, chances are you'd take a camera to take pictures so you could remember the experience afterward. Many people take cameras on their vacations. Would you take an old box camera with a fixed lens and black and white film or the newest color videotape, slide, or film camera with automatic and zoom lenses? Silly question? Many interviewers and interrogators use themselves as an old black-and-white box camera. They see others through the smudged lens of their own prejudice, through the outdated film of their own limited education, training, and life experience. Most of the time they aren't even aware of it. They see as St. Paul said "as through a glass, darkly." Some of us see only half the truth, some see only a fraction of the truth. Some never see the truth at all. When sworn in, in every court across the land, you raise your right hand, the other on a Bible, and swear to tell "the truth, the whole truth and nothing but the truth, so help you God." As you will see in this chapter, that's far more difficult than it sounds.

The title of this book, *Interview and Interrogation, A Scientific Approach*, is intended to **constantly** remind you that in order to see the truth **every** interview, **every** interrogation must be done **scientifically.** You must be not only a skilled "people detective" in the tradition of Sherlock Holmes, but also an experimental scientist, practicing your questioning craft in carefully controlled, closely monitored laboratory conditions. This requires a thorough knowledge of yourself, to use yourself as a camera, with a clean lens and fresh untouched film. In 600 BC, the simple 2-word still timely message was inscribed over the door of the Greek temple of Delphi: "Know thyself." To be a **scientific** interviewer and interrogator you must be aware of and understand yourself **before** you see or question anyone. This book is intended to develop skills in an orderly, **scientific way**, starting with a study of yourself. Jumping around, using only parts of this book or moving too quickly, is like using a camera in too big a hurry. You are bound to get fuzzy, incomplete pictures. Stop now as you read this sentence and promise yourself to move slowly, carefully, through these pages.

Why examine yourself before you question others? If you were physically or sexually abused as a child and are questioning the victim or the suspect, will you be as objective and unmoved with both of them? If you were the child of alcoholics and are interviewing a drunk, will your contact be the same as with a nonalcoholic? If a suspect is of a different race, sex, or nationality, could an observer see any difference in your questioning style? If you are a Vietnam veteran and are interrogating another Nam veteran will you be as objective as for a nonveteran? Generally, do you question men, women, gays—perhaps AIDS victims— without **any** emotional involvement, all in the same way, "strictly business?" It's doubtful. The purpose of this chapter is to increase your awareness of psychological and emotional "unfinished business" that can interfere with your effectiveness as a scientific interviewer or interrogator. There are many more interfering factors and forces than you may have realized.

From the instant of conception, you developed from one to millions of cells, from a tiny baby to your present age and size. At **every step** along the way you were conditioned by thousands of situations and factors much like a bullet which picks up markings and scratches from the barrel. The first such "mark" on your personality was the **instant of conception**. It determined your sex, race, and gene pool for intelligence and inherent or native abilities. Those were all nature's "gifts" to you through your parents. In addition, there were **environmental factors** placed on you well before your birth. If your mother smoked excessively, abused alcohol or drugs, or had a serious infectious illness, these could have affected you before, during, and after your birth. Many criminals have a **lifelong history** of problems, starting with being a sickly child, abused by others, often complicated by poverty, social isolation, and lack of opportunity. None of these, of course, justify a life of crime. A son, facing serious charges, complained to his father: "Y'know, Pop, I never asked to be born." The father replied: "Well, maybe if you hadda asked, the answer mighta been 'No!' "

Some behavioral experts feel that **difficult or prolonged labor** can influence early personality development. The psychiatrist, Otto Rank, one of Freud's colleagues, taught that the trauma of birth is the first life shock or trauma, being forcibly expelled from the safety, warmth, and comfort of the womb. Nobody asks you if you're ready for the trip! Shakespeare described this in his play *MacBeth* as being "plucked untimely from the womb." The famous psychiatrist, Karl Menninger, considered birth to be a powerful influence on personality from the moment you are held upside down and given a spank to dislodge mucus from your mouth: "Swallow it and you're an introvert; spit it out and you're an extrovert." A psychiatric mental status examination includes a question about complications at birth. Some experts feel they can result in lowered resistance to disease, chronic or congenital conditions, weight extremes, or emotional problems and depression, irritability, even violence if reinforced later by family or life situations. Your own birth is the first major change in your own life experience. It can be an important step in the overall design of yourself as a camera. How was it for you? What did your mother or family tell you about it? How could it have influenced you physically and personally?

Purely **genetic factors** can and do play a role in any interaction and especially in interview and interrogation.

Racial and sex differences are important genetic factors. If they separate you from others they become an influence on how you perceive yourself and others. Treated as inferior long enough, you will consider yourself to be inferior. If you are in a minority status by race or even sex (a woman who wanders into an exclusively men's club or vice versa) you will certainly be noticed and are likely to be viewed with suspicion. What you are wearing and how you behave will add to or diminish the suspicion. If there have been racial problems, demonstrations, or riots, anyone in that minority group can be in danger from the majority. Majority persons who happen in or near large groups from the minority are also in a high-risk situation. The color of one's skin makes it easier to separate that person from others. This has been true of American Indians, Blacks, and those from the Middle and Far East, Arabic peoples, Chinese, Japanese, etc.

Sex can be a factor which influences attitude and behavior. The terms **male chauvinist, feminist, bitch, fag,** or **queer** are but a few of many negative references to sex or sexual preference. Until the Korean War, the Marine Corps was an all white (Caucasian) organization. Like all branches of the military, it is now integrated not only by race but also by sex. Interestingly, there were women Marines before blacks were allowed to join. In some settings and situations, the old prejudices are still felt, but they are fading as men and women of all races work together and realize they are more similar than different. If a person of any other race is injured, red blood flows, just as it would if you were cut. Racial, age, and sexist prejudice, can be important factors in psychological and social development. You should be aware of what these factors mean to you in terms of your age, race, and sex.

Dr. Leo Kanner, an internationally known child psychiatrist, taught that the single most important function of parents in the first five years of a child's life was simply to **keep the child alive.** Stated another way, the first priority is to give children **safety** and **security.** Next in importance, according to Dr. Kanner, is to give children "the three A's" of **approval, acceptance,** and **affection.** Do these, he said, and there is no need to read books or take courses on how to raise children, nor to worry about how good a parent you are. Infancy and early childhood, that period from birth to the school years, is an important stage of life. By the time you are five years old you have absorbed 25,000 hours of programmed instruction from your parents, according to transactional analysis theory, a way of analyzing human interaction. The quality of parent-to-child and family relations, and the quality of the home setting—warmth, safety, clothing, nutrition, comfort—are important influences on children.

It is during **infancy** and **early childhood** that many children are exposed to and learn negative behaviors. **Parental relations** can have negative impact on children's personality development if they are inconsistent or erratic, overprotective, too permissive, blaming or critical, perfectionistic, indifferent, play favorites, or are absent totally or for long periods of time. Parents are **role models** and if one or both are alcoholics or drug abusers, the child learns that one way to cope with stress is to drink or take drugs. The same is true for smoking. Worse still, there is a correlation between abusing parents and being abused as children. Many child abusers grow up to become child abusers themselves. A violent, disruptive home life can be a school for violence and aggressive behavior. "Spare the rod and spoil the child" and "children should be seen and not heard," if applied strictly, teach physical abuse as the best way to control behavior and passive, dependent silence as the best way for children to behave. As the Old Testament put it: "Train up a child in the way he should go and when he is old he will not depart from it" (Proverbs 22:6). A standard part of a mental status examination is to ask if the person interviewed had a happy childhood. How was yours? It's yet another factor in your own personality formation.

National and ethnic differences can be major influences if they separate you from others, such as living in a ghetto or an ethnic section of the community. The musical *Fiddler on the Roof* is based on the dilemma of Jewish customs and tradition in a changing society. Another popular musical, *West Side Story,* focusses on friction between Hispanics and whites. Shakespeare's *Romeo and Juliet* was a similar theme based on two feuding Italian families. Two movies, available on videotape, describe the interaction of different cultures: *Lawrence of Arabia,* starring Peter O'Toole, Omar Sharif, and Claude Rains, and *Khartoum,* with Charlton Heston and Sir Laurence Olivier. Viewing these film classics is an excellent way to study differences in culture, politics, motivation, personality, and behavior. Today we have a weaker but still observable caste system based on income or wealth, occupation or position, social status, and family.

Regional differences can have an influence on attitude and behavior. Brightly colored shirts or blouses are common in Hawaii but not downtown at midday in most midcontinent cities. Restaurants feature "regional specialties" on their menus. You can still hear regional dialects. **Caudal** does not mean **tail** in the deep South, but what the gas station attendant tells you: your car needs "A caud all" (quart of oil). A **tar** is a tire, **wahr** is wire, and **woah** is war. In Boston, to buy on credit you need a fresh fish! They'll ask for your **credit cod.** They may even ask if you want to go to the **potty** (party)! Tourist bureaus promote regional customs, traditions, foods, history, culture, and natural resources.

Unless you were born into a large family, school is your first close social experience. Your favorite toys, perhaps an old worn security blanket, and the safety and comfort of your home are left behind to go to a big building with many other children and obey a stranger who tells you what to do. It is at this stage that some develop problems relating to authority figures. Some children have panic reactions, are frightened and upset, and develop a "school phobia." Others become manipulators learning devious ways to have their way, apprentice con artists. Still others learn they can have their way by beating up on others, especially the weaker ones. Some feel safer and more secure with their own racial, religious, ethnic, or neighborhood group, and gangs form. For most children, the school years encourage social behaviors, learning basic knowledge about their own unique interests and abilities.

School years provide peer relations, contact and interaction with boys and girls outside the family. Children and teenagers are very much into their own group norms. They wear the same fashions, eat the same foods, listen to the same music. In most cases their taste differs markedly from parents and older brothers and sisters. Drug abuse, gangs, and cults are negative group norms for many teenagers. Can you remember your teen years? For most of us it was a search for ourselves, who we were, what would become of us, whether anyone would ever love us, if we would ever live to the very old age of 21! Remember those brooding, worrisome thoughts? **Teen years** are often an awkward time. If there have been continuing negative influences from early childhood, antisocial and violent behaviors can be further reinforced in the teens. It is in the teen years that many careers in crime begin.

Your **first sexual experience** can have a marked effect on your future relationships with the opposite sex. Men who can't perform sexually (often according to their own unrealistic expectations) can develop long-standing problems with sexual relations. The same is true for women who have been raped or where sex was forced on them. Some men and women learn that sex is a way of manipulating others, as a reward or a conquest, not a shared exchange of affection. Some men see women only as sex objects. Some women see sex as a man's "Achilles' heel" and use it to control and dominate men. In an ancient Greek comedy, women joined together and denied sex with the men until the men agreed never to wage war. Many men don't consider that to be a comedy! Still other men and women learn "kinky" sex is about all they can get, so some men are "turned on" by children and some women by bondage or being physically or verbally abused. Sex is a powerful drive and if it isn't vented in socially accepted ways, it can become a negative force in personality development.

Religion can influence behavior. Ayatollah Khomeini was an Islamic religious leader who condemned America as "the Great Satan" and condoned terrorism and hostage-taking. Catholics and Protestants in northern Ireland regularly shoot at each other or at the local police or British security forces, "open season" targets for both sides. Hindu and Islamic peoples fought each other before Pakistan became independent of India. Though we do not kill because of religion, sectarian differences have resulted in much prejudice, friction, distrust, and hurt feelings.

Your **choice of occupation** can influence behavior. Construction workers are frequently shown with hard hats and leather tool belts ogling at women. Police officers are considered largely conservative, social workers as "bleeding heart liberals." Psychiatrists and psychologists can seem "fuzzy headed" when they disagree on seemingly simple cases (such as when Hinckley shot President Reagan). Some say that "a smart lawyer can get anyone off free." These are extreme statements, not necessarily true. But your choice of career **can** influence your attitude, your values, what you believe, and what you say and do. Police officers **do** tend to distrust others because every day they observe people who violate the law. Bank personnel tend to be conservative when it comes to managing money. Perhaps Ebenezer Scrooge in Charles Dickens' **Christmas Carol** is a good example of how a stingy man becomes a narrow, rigid personality. Freud called such people **anal retentive**—they "hold it in." Psychotherapists tend to give people "the benefit of the doubt," to "explain away behaviors" because that is their business, what they do for and with their clients.

Marriage is a major change in anyone's life, from living alone (in most cases!) to living with someone else. It is sharing your life with someone else, far more intimately than in any family situation, or even a roommate at college, or sharing an apartment. It means shared finances, friends, food, bills, quirks, sex, and life. Some people marry similar personalities, others marry opposites. Some marry those much like their own parents or family members, others pursue those most unlike anyone they know. Some marry to escape the single life or their family, others to find security, like Gershwin's tune, *Someone to watch over me.* Children of alcoholics frequently marry alcoholics. Some marry in the naive attempt to reform or rehabilitate the spouse. Your choice of husband or wife and the nature of the relationship in your marriage is a powerful influence on your life and on your personality. The ideal marriage is $1 + 1 = 3$, where you both gain or grow more than you could alone. Is it so for you? How's your marriage? How are **you** because of it?

The Vietnam War has proven that **military experience,** especially in a combat situation, can affect personality and behavior. This is true for all wars. What we now call **post-traumatic stress disorder** has been reported in the Revolutionary and Civil wars, World Wars I and II, and the Korean War. A similar "psychological wound" can be inflicted with any shock such as child abuse, rape, accident, natural catastrophe, or loss of a loved one or a limb, sight, or hearing. Severe stress from any of these sources impacts on thoughts and feelings and can intrude and interfere with healthy personality development.

What have you learned from this quick trip through your life? Summing up, there can be powerful physical and mental forces from birth to death that shape personality, like a rifle bullet picking up markings along the barrel. Each of us is as unique as a bullet, with distinctive markings and life scratches. No one else is quite the same. Even another bullet fired from the same weapon will differ because of its own individual materials and shape. To understand others, to know what they think and feel, in an interview or interrogation, you must first understand yourself, what and how you think and feel.

EXERCISE 1

Here are the factors and forces that have had an effect on you, have helped shape your personality and behavior. Write them down or photocopy this list and reflect on each of them. What effect or influence do you think each factor had on you? What adverse effect could it have on your ability to clearly, openly see and understand the truth when questioning others? You may find it helpful to keep a record or file, a diary or journal of your reaction to each of the exercises in this book. In this way, you can more easily see what you have learned from each chapter and in personal terms, especially meaningful to you.

Birth (genes; complications; diseases)
Race (minority or majority)
Sex, sexism (it is a man's world)
Infancy and early childhood
National and/or ethnic differences
Family relations
Home (security, wealth, poverty)
Social status/standing, expectations
Regional influences
School experience
Friends, brothers, sisters
Physical health
Sexual experience and preference
Religious affiliation, differences
Occupation
Marriage
Financial problems

Managing children
Military experience
Loss and stress

Life Stages

Erik Erikson (1902–) described eight life stages. At each stage it is as if you are at a fork in the road of life and must choose one way to go. You can't go back, and you can't try them both. Once on the path, what happens influences your behavior and your personality. Here they are:

Stage 1. Basic Trust or Mistrust?

You're wet and hungry, crying in your crib, totally dependent on a certain giant person who feeds and clothes you and sometimes holds you and makes sounds. If that person doesn't appear regularly or lets you cry and be uncomfortable, you learn distrust. If you feel good and are dry and well fed most of the time, you learn to trust.

Stage 2. Autonomy or Shame and Doubt.

At this stage you walk, talk, and "go potty," but these are new experiences, and you're not too sure of yourself. You gotta know when to hold it and when to let go, do or not to do. Screw up and there's shame and self-doubt. Master it and you really feel satisfied and confident.

Stage 3. Initiate or Guilt?

You're exploring, experimenting, playing with everything, including your own body. Wups! It feels good but you get smacked. Learn what's "good" and "bad" and you continue on adjusting to realities. Keep getting punished and you're on a guilt trip.

Stage 4. Industry or Inferiority?

It's Erector sets or doll houses, scrawly drawings and messy crafts with increased self-confidence if successful ("Wow, look what I did!") or low self-esteem and inferiority if not.

Stage 5. Identity or Role Diffusion?

The four preceding stages flow into this one, where you realize more fully than ever before who you are (ego identity) by comparing yourself with others. This is also what we're trying to do to you with this chapter!

Stage 6. Intimacy or Isolation?

It is here the love bug bites you, but good! It's close friends sharing intimate secrets, that "first love" and perhaps your first sexual experience. If the relationship goes well, you feel good about yourself and others and continue. If not, you withdraw and become a loner or just sit wishing someone would call.

Stage 7. Generativity or Stagnation?

Class, church, clubs, hobbies, even raising children fall into this stage. It is doing something because you care, making a contribution, making a difference. Frustrated here, you drop out and stagnate, a leading cause of burnout.

Stage 8. Ego Integrity or Despair?

This is the self-actualization stage where you can feel personally fulfilled, a whole person, receptive and accepting of self and others, an OK person able to love and be loved just being you. You can't get here without insight, wisdom, and a little humor. Miss this and the road leads down to depression and despair, the feeling that somehow you missed out on life, and life missed you.

Some behavioral scientists believe that you have within you a potential for strength and stability to overcome negative factors and forces. Some of us do. Some of us don't—and resort to antisocial or illegal acts to make up for misfortune. For most of us, this real or authentic self is by its nature positive, optimistic, and healthy. It has its own sense of values, what is right and what is wrong for you and for others, which is most like the **Golden Rule,** to do to others what you would want them to do to you. The psychologist Abraham Maslow described this healthy, well adjusted personality as **self-actualized,** with need levels to be satisfied:

Maslow's Need Levels

1. PHYSIOLOGICAL NEEDS: To be kept dry, warm and fed, clothed and sheltered, comforted and cuddled.
2. SECURITY: To be safe, free from danger, from sudden shocks and injuries.

3. EMOTIONAL SUPPORT: The "apronstrings" stage, the need for someone to watch over you, to be with as if to give you permission to be yourself and "do your thing."
4. APPROVAL: This involves acceptance, belonging, fellow feeling and can be seen in fads, cliques, clubs, teams, or gangs. Very strong in teen years.
5. FULFILLMENT: Self-realization, to realize your true self and your potential. Adulthood "becoming." Can be buying a new home, car, or suit, rearranging furniture, repainting a room, changing jobs, or the Nobel prize!

EXERCISE 2

Physical, mental, and emotional factors at each life stage and need level shape personality. Before you can know and understand the personalities and behaviors of others, you must know and understand your own. Only in this way can you function as a camera, with clean lens and fresh, untouched film. To help understand yourself, review Erikson's life stages, then Maslow's need levels, and write down any experiences and situations that may have blocked or frustrated your fully realizing them. Consider how they might now influence what you see in others as you question them?

The Scientific Method

To become a **scientific** interviewer or interrogator, you must have a working knowledge of **the scientific method**. It is the 5-step method shared by all the sciences, worldwide, from Aristotle to Einstein. No great advance in science has ever been achieved without it. It is based on careful attention to detail, objective observation, and systematic analysis of all available information in an open, free search for truth. The British biologist, physician, and teacher, Thomas Huxley (1825–1895), described the scientific method as "trained and organized common sense, rigidly accurate in observation and merciless to fallacy in logic." In his book, *The Life of Reason,* the philosopher George Santayana (1863–1952) described it as "developed perception, interpreted intent, common sense rounded out and minutely articulated." The great physicist Albert Einstein considered science to be a reflection of reality and truth, and he defined the scientific method as "to cover the greatest number of empirical facts by logical deduction from the smallest number of hypotheses and axioms." All of these definitions apply as well to **scientific** interview and interrogation.

A **scientific** approach to interview and interrogation is to consider every contact with another person as would a careful researcher. Justice Oliver Wendell Holmes, in his U.S. Supreme Court opinion in the *Abrams vs U.S.* case in 1919, wrote that "all life is an experiment." Human personality and behavior **are** fascinating to observe and study. Hans Selye, an international authority on stress and its effects, commented: "The true scientist never loses the faculty of amazement. It is the essence of his being."

Here are the five steps of the scientific method, shared by all what world's sciences, from ancient times to the next issue of scientific journals:

Step 1. State the Problem/Goal. Define Terms.
(Draw and redraw a map)

Be honest (nobody's watching!) and take a good, hard look at yourself (no pain, no gain!) before answering this next question. How many times have you been in a disagreement with someone only to discover the problem was caused by a misunderstanding? One or both of you **assumed** something that wasn't true? You learned the hard way that to **assume** is to make an **ass** out of **you** and **me** (ass/u/me). Before you can debate with anyone, have a free give-and-take exchange of differing opinions, both sides have to understand the basic premise and agree on definitions and ground rules. Otherwise it could become total confusion. Before lawyers go to court they must know which laws apply and have a clear understanding of what those laws mean. Even in court, the case proceeds under the watchful eye of the judge who ensures everyone understands and follows the same rules.

You cannot be an effective interviewer or interrogator unless and until you can clearly see what it is you are doing. That may sound simple, but you would be shocked and amazed to see how many interviews ramble on like a ship without a rudder because the questioner does not fully, clearly understand the purpose, the goal, the end result sought. You can drive your car to the store by turning left or right or choosing one street over another but the target, the purpose, the reason for the trip is to go to the store. Before you interview or interrogate anyone, you must first take as much time as needed to reflect and agree on your goal or purpose. WHAT is it you are doing? WHY are you doing it? Carefully study this. Revise it as needed to sharpen the focus. The foundation of any questioning session must be carefully laid before you ever see the other person, even before you begin collecting background information.

Step 2. Observe Objectively.
(Be a camera)

This step enables you to see what's there (like a camera), not what you want to see (through your own tinted glasses), not what you have been conditioned or learned to see (through your own life experience). To achieve this, you must cancel out, neutralize, transcend your own physical and mental "unfinished business." A camera doesn't think or feel. It gives you a candid, precise picture fixed in time, exactly at the instant the photo was taken. Truth is like that. It exists regardless of what **you** think or feel about it. The best interviewers and interrogators see the truth even though it might disagree with their own beliefs, experience, or expectations. Like skilled surgeons, they observe clearly and objectively despite their own attitude and values, whether the persons questioned are rapists, murderers, or even job applicants who "turn them off." As cameras, their lenses are clear and untinted.

Oliver Wendell Holmes, the medical professor, preached to his students the importance of objective observation. One day, just before lunch, he displayed a clear glass beaker full of urine from a diabetic patient. "I want you all to line up in a single file," he said, "and come up here and do as I do." He put a finger into the beaker, then lifted his hand to his face and touched his tongue. "In the field," he explained, "far from laboratories, you will have to use quick, informal spot tests. You will notice a distinctive sweet taste to the urine. Come and do as you saw me do." One at a time, each student passed before the beaker and did as they were told, returning to their seats looking and feeling queasy. "Now," Professor Holmes said, "if you did what you saw me do you would have observed that I put my index finger into the beaker but my middle finger to my tongue! How many times have I told you to **observe objectively?**"

Objectivity means a free, open search for truth, without bias or preconceived notion, interpretation, or opinion. Alfred Kinsey, author of the first major study of human sexual behavior, summed it up well: "We are recorders and reporters of the facts, not judges of the behavior we describe." In **scientific** interview and interrogation, to paraphrase an old saying, yours is not to reason why but to find out **when, what, who,** and **how.** A healthy skepticism, not sarcasm or cynicism, helps preserve objectivity when questioning others. "Truth is stranger than fiction, believe half of what you hear, nothing is certain, things are seldom what they seem" are all old sayings which recommend remaining open and objective. It also helps to realize you don't know everything. No one does. Socrates defined intelligence as knowing what you don't know. Tom Edison once said that "we don't know one millionth of one percent about anything." In his musical *Porgy and Bess,* George Gershwin wrote a song for skeptics: *It ain't necessarily so.* The Bible tells us to "prove all things," and some of Buddha's dying words were: "Test all truth, take nothing for granted." The lesson from all these sources, ancient to modern: See what's there, not what you want to see or expect to see. Be like the railroad crossing sign: **Stop. Look. Listen.**

How observant are you? You've seen McDonald's fast food restaurant signs all along the interstate highways on those blue and white signs. McDonald's registered trademark is a red background with a yellow M (the "golden arches") and the name "McDonald's" in white letters. But is the name centered across the bottom of the yellow M, or off center to the left or right? Chevron gas stations use how many chevrons in their sign—two or three? What colors? Which color is the chevron on the top? Does the sign have all capital letters or caps and lower case? Is the vertical line making up the left side of the H on Holiday Inn signs straight (vertical) or curved? Does it lean to the left or right? You've seen these signs many times but have you **really** seen them?

Think this is nitpicking? Trivia? As World War II was ending, an allied soldier routinely stopped a truck full of weary Italian soldiers at a roadblock. He observed a man in a worn sergeant's overcoat. Nothing unusual, except that his boots were polished and looked expensive. Everyone else wore muddied, worn shoes or boots. The allied soldier had apprehended Benito Mussolini. That one minor detail cost Mussolini his life. Attention to detail is a vital part of interview and interrogation.

Step 3. Gather Data. Accumulate Information
(Be a computer database, a sponge)

This step links you as a camera with you as a computer. To master this step requires that you accumulate as much information as possible, leaving nothing out, facts and opinions, hard evidence or theories, "working hypotheses." This is best done without manipulating or even arranging the information but rather just piling it up. Gathering data is like collecting a good library of every reference you can find on a subject. **Before** they explain a phenomenon, scientists first **gather data,** in this same way. The psychiatrist, Carl G. Jung, had a personal library of 100,000 books. Sigmund Freud collected 1000 dreams before he wrote his analysis of dream interpretation. Tom Edison did 10,000 experiments before he discovered the secret of a simple light bulb.

Like scientists, expert interviewers and interrogators let the data take them where it will. They keep accumulating information and in time the weight of the data moves in certain directions. The scientist simply follows the information or "paper trail" as a hunting dog follows a scent. Some are dead ends, others lead to still more information, more directions. This does not require much thought. Too much thinking can force you off the trail. Be a computer. As some experts say, computers are "dumb." They only "know" what you "tell" them, what you put into them. They only store information. That is what the 3rd step of the scientific method requires of **you**.

Here are some examples of how gathering data has paid off. During World War II, censors opened and read mail and tapped phone lines to keep sensitive information from falling into enemy hands. By assembling bits of information from many letters, it was possible to trace a trade route that led to the sinking of seven enemy cargo ships. A letter from a mother in Europe to her son in America assured him when he returned he could take the train to work. This signalled completion of a railroad line which was promptly bombed. In the United States alone there were 15,000 censors who could read 300 languages, proof of the importance of gathering data (*Reader's Digest,* 1964).

Step 4. Evaluate. Sift. Creative play.
    (Be a blank slate, an empty pitcher.)

It is at this 4th step—and **only** at this step—that you allow your brain to shift into gear, to sift through your storehouse of information and arrange it into patterns. Now you allow yourself to be influenced by the data. This is a very delicate phase because if you haven't neutralized your own mental "unfinished business" or "hidden agenda" you can be led astray and make serious mistakes. There have been tragic injustices throughout history when people have "rushed to judgment." The great philosopher Socrates was tried by a jury in peace-loving Athens, convicted and executed for "corrupting youth." Jesus was tried, convicted, tortured, and killed by due process of the same Roman Empire that produced Cicero and Julius Caesar. As Norman Vincent Peale wrote: "Twist the truth and make a hit. Tell the truth and get hit." It is at this 4th step you are no longer "dumb" as a camera or computer but "smart" as a Sherlock Holmes. That legendary master detective was a skilled observer, carefully attentive to detail, and sharply perceptive, the ideal blend for the most effective interview and interrogation.

As a general rule, the more you have learned and know about life and people, the more you have experienced yourself, the sharper is your perception **into** and **through** people. It is as Zen Buddhists teach, that you "see with the third eye and hear with the third ear." On the other hand, if your knowledge and experience of yourself and others is limited, your perception will be distorted, unclear, and misleading.

Step 5. Conclusions. Decide. Explain.
(Be an Olympics judge)

At this final step interviewers determine whether or not the applicant gets the job or that the right information has been obtained. Interrogators decide whether or not the suspect should be charged or the **real** truth of what happened, when, how, by whom. If you master and use all five steps of the scientific method, your observations and the information you collected will lead you to a conclusion. Like scientists, the data will lead you on the road to truth despite side streets and distracting trails, like a river that flows wider and faster in one direction despite misleading smaller streams. As the old saying goes: "The truth will out."

Intelligence, the ability to think clearly, to "work smart" facilitates this final step. Without clear, logical, bright thinking all of your previous work can end in error. It is like Homer and Jethro on their first ride on a train. They were fascinated with the sounds and the sights along the way. A vendor came through the car selling fruit. They had never seen a banana and they each bought one. Homer pulled back the skin as the vendor instructed him and took a bite. At that instant the train went through a long tunnel and everything went black. "Uh, Jethro," Homer said anxiously, "you et your'n yet?" Jethro answered: "No, I ain't." "Well," Homer said, "don't do it. I just took a bite of mine and the damn thing blinded me!" All the observation and information in the world won't help you if you can't evaluate and explain it.

Try to make sense, to get any meaning, from these words:

THAT THAT IS IS

Until you add punctuation it's nonsense:

THAT, THAT IS, IS!

Yes, everything that exists indeed **does exist!**

Or this one: GODISNOWHERE

Spaced two different ways it is the defiant statement of an atheist: GOD IS NOWHERE. Or it is the prayerful perception of the devoutly religious: GOD IS NOW HERE. Both statements are opposite in meaning yet look identical. The truth is not always obvious. As Gilbert and Sullivan wrote in *HMS Pinafore*, "things are seldom what they seem; skim milk masquerades as cream." To be objective, to analyze scientifically, we would have to say that neither statement can be proven with 100 percent certainty. Both statements are **unscientific** for that reason. To make them acceptable, you would have to add clarification, such as: "Some people believe that God is nowhere" or "some people believe that God is here, now, in their everyday lives." To be **really** scientific though, we'd have to define the terms **some** (how many are some?) and **people** (all people worldwide, historically or just currently?).

EXERCISE 3

Consider how you would use the five steps of the scientific method in order to:

(a) buy a new car
(b) buy a new suit or dress
(c) choose new wallpaper or interior paint color
(d) choose your next vacation place and length of time
(e) choose what you will have for lunch tomorrow

After you have done these, review what you have done. How does it differ from the way you have chosen before? Is doing it this way an improvement? Less impulsive, better reasoned? If so, **that** is the **value** of the scientific method. It also shows you how **unscientific** you have been in the past!

EXERCISE 4

Evaluate and reach a conclusion about these statements. Decide whether each statement is scientific or unscientific, then whether it is true, false, a half truth, or mostly true, or mostly false. If unscientific, how could you reword it to be more scientific? Which words require more definition?

1. All politicians are crooked.
2. There's a Ford in your future.
3. Where there's smoke there's fire.
4. Never give a sucker an even break.
5. Better to be safe than sorry.
6. No pain, no gain.
7. Gentlemen prefer blondes.
8. Diamonds are a girl's best friend.
9. Use it or lose it.
10. It always rains on vacation.
11. Time flies when you're having fun.
12. Frenchmen are good lovers.
13. Women are catty (are men doggy?).
14. This dozen eggs are rotten because this one's rotten.
15. Mary is not married; she is therefore an unfit mother.
16. You have 24-hour virus, because that's how I felt when I had it.
17. Everyone has his or her price.
18. What goes up must come down.
19. Every saint is a sinner.
20. Haste makes waste.
21. The criminal returns to the scene of the crime.

EXERCISE 5

Here are some quotes to analyze in the same way:

1. "Science is simply common sense at its best—rigidly accurate in observation and merciless to fallacy in logic" (T. X. Huxley).
2. "Science is nothing but developed perception, interpreted intent, common sense rounded-out and minutely articulated" (George Santayana).
3. "Science is the systematic classification of experience" (George Henry Lewes).
4. "Science is organized knowledge" (Edmund Spencer)
5. "Science is nothing but perception" (Plato).
6. "You can't see any further into a generalization than your knowledge of its details" (William James).
7. "No generalization is worth a damn—including this one" (Oliver Wendell Holmes).

8. "Beware of advice—even this!" (Carl Sandburg)
9. "Know thyself" (Plutarch).
10. "There's a sucker born every minute" (P. T. Barnum).

WHAT HAVE YOU LEARNED?

There were two goals in this chapter. The first goal was to introduce you **to yourself**, to help you see inside yourself for thoughts or feelings, mental "unfinished business" that can interfere with your understanding another person. The many factors from birth **to this very minute** that could have impacted on you physically or emotionally to shape your present attitude and behavior were described and listed. In the exercises you were asked to examine these factors. If you haven't done so, stop now and go back (what the hell's the hurry, anyway?). The time will be well spent—unless and until you can neutralize your own prejudice and preconceived notions you will forever see others through tinted glasses, a camera with a smudged lens.

The second major goal was to introduce you to the scientific method, the 5-step process shared by all the sciences. How this worldwide, time-tested method applies to interview and interrogation was described. Exercises gave you the opportunity to scientifically analyze sayings and statements and how you yourself use or do not use it to choose products and services.

PLEASE do NOT go on to the next chapter until you feel you have mastered these two goals and thoroughly understand them. The next chapter will describe normal and abnormal behaviors and how to apply the scientific method to observe and analyze them. You won't fully understand it unless your own eyes (camera lens and computer screen) are clear.

Chapter 2

THEM: WHO ARE THEY?

What you are shouts so loudly
I can't hear a word you're saying
Ralph Waldo Emerson

WHAT'S NORMAL?

Everybody has a personality. The psychologist Gordon Allport once counted more than 50 different definitions of personality in scientific books and journals (1937). Even today there is no universally accepted definition. For our purpose in preparing you to be an expert interviewer or interrogator, personality is the totality of your being and includes physical factors (age, height, weight, nutrition, health, appearance, and grooming) and mental factors (intelligence, memory, attitudes, and motivation, thoughts, and feelings). Physical factors are genetic and bio-chemical, though poor nutrition and diseases any time in life are also physical factors. Mental factors are mostly learned but some, such as intelligence, are actually genetic. So there is much overlap between what is physical and what is mental. Years ago it was debated which was more important, heredity or environment. They're both important. Personality changes with life experience and aging. As the old Alaska sourdough said: "I ain't what I wanna be and I ain't what I'm gonna be, but I sure as hell ain't what I used to be."

Over the last hundred years many personality theories have become popular then faded into obscurity. Most of them grew from three major theories and being familiar with them will help you understand human nature and sharpen your questioning skills.

PSYCHOANALYTIC THEORY

Sigmund Freud 1856–1937

Freud was a physician and most medical schools and psychiatric training reflects his theory which he named **psychoanalysis.** He called the basic life force the **libido** (lib-ee-doe). When it is invested in thoughts, feelings, people, or things it is called a **cathexis.** Freud taught that the mind is like an iceberg, most of it below the surface. This submerged content he called **the unconscious.** It is beyond reach of the conscious mind except by therapy or interpreting dreams.

Personality consists of three **ego states:** the **id,** your dark side, "the beast within," primitive and instinctual, irrational, fantasy-dominated, and pleasure seeking; the **superego,** your conscience, values, restrictions and controls; the **ego,** the rational, moderating, reality testing part of you. Personality is a dynamic balance of these three states, the interplay and interaction of them. Think longingly about a hot fudge sundae (the id will help you) but realize you're on a diet (courtesy of your superego) then decide that right now it's better not to have one (voice of the ego). Wanna have sex (id asks)? If you're married (superego specifies) you could ask or make your usual move (ego facilitates). Criminals have little or no superego controlling their motives and, in addition, usually low ego strength, resulting in id dominating and resultant impulsive or violent behaviors.

According to Freudian theory, personality develops through five stages:

ORAL: Sucking and swallowing, from birth 'til weaning, but thumbsucking, nailbiting, and later chewing gum, smoking and drinking beer from bottles are leftovers of this infantile behavior.

ANAL: At about age 2, seated on the potty, you learn there are times to "hold it" and times to "let it go." Prior to that time it was great fun just letting go. Talkative people ("verbal diarrhea") or stingy Scrooge-like people ("anal retentive") are still sitting on the pot. If you think this is far fetched, why do people say "Oh shit!" or "I don't give a shit"? Those are references to anal activity.

PHALLIC: In early childhood, boys attach to mother and resent father (**Oedipus complex**) but fear reprisal (**castration** anxiety). Girls attach to father and resent mother (**Electra complex**) but are frustrated because they can't have father's penis (**penis envy**).

LATENCY: This is a dormant stage usually age 7–12 when the sex drive is on hold, what Freud called a period of "infantile amnesia" when you forget about the phallic pleasures you had earlier.

GENITAL: Puberty! The hormones flow and the id rises to the occasion in starry-eyed watching the opposite sex, awkward talk and behaviors between them, fads and fears, wet dreams, and moodiness. Then it's on to adulthood.

To learn more about Freudian theory, see the Alfred Hitchcock movie *Spellbound* starring Gregory Peck and Ingrid Bergman. It's a good short course in psychoanalytic theory and practice. After that, try *Lovesick* with Arthur Moore, Elizabeth McGovern, and Alec Guinness as the ghost of Freud. It's a lighthearted spoof of Freudian theory. Both are available from videotape film rental outlets.

BEHAVIORIST THEORY

Ivan Pavlov (1849–1936); B. F. Skinner (1904–)

Ivan Petrovich Pavlov was a Russian physiologist who experimented with the salivation reflex in dogs. He served meat and the dogs salivated. Nothing new. He served meat and rang a bell and the dogs salivated. Then he rang the bell but without meat—and the dogs salivated. This was the first experimental evidence for conditioning. If you can do it with dogs, why not with people? In the United States, the psychologist, Clark Hull (1884–1952), continued Pavlov's work, adding the **Stimulus-Response** or S–R sequence. Hull saw responses to stimuli as reducing instinctive drives. Given a choice, the animal or the person chooses the most pleasurable, less painful response and will submit to pain to experience pleasure. Behaviorism considers avoiding pain and pursuing pleasure to be a very strong, basic motivation.

The term **behaviorism** was first used in 1913 by John Broadus Watson. It was at that time Freudian theories were widely discussed and debated. Watson openly opposed Freudian theory which he considered subjective and unscientific. B. F. Skinner (1902–) enlarged behaviorist theory when in 1953 he described the **functional analysis of behavior,** where behavior and environmental events are defined and analyzed by their effect on each other. Past (**antecedent**) and present (**consequent**) behaviors are studied as to frequency, duration, intensity, and time. Conditions are then manipulated to change outcome (**shaping**). This is done by careful selection and use of **reinforcers.** These methods have proven effective in the treatment of phobias, habit control, thought stopping, and toilet training of the mentally retarded.

Cues are opportunities to react. A lone woman or child in a dark or secluded place can be the cue for robbery, rape or kidnapping. **Reinforcement** is the repetition of an S–R sequence into a pattern. Habits like nailbiting, gum chewing, and smoking become habits by being repeated and relieving tension, a form of pleasure. Alcohol and drug abuse are reinforced by continuing to take them but also because they insulate you from painful reality or get you high, forms of pleasure. Many rapists and child abusers and all serial killers are repeat offenders, suggesting that these violent acts are reinforced.

B. F. Skinner is the leading proponent of behaviorism today. His version is called **operant conditioning** and is based on the theory that people can exhibit spontaneous behaviors without a specific stimulus. He calls them **operants** and has developed a wide array of reinforcement methods. Pavlov reinforced the stimulus. Skinner reinforces the response. He introduced **successive approximation,** a way of **shaping** behavior by tiny steps.

Behaviorists contend that most, perhaps all behavior is learned. Personality is formed, shaped, like a ball of putty, by life experience that functions like a series of experiments. The world is the laboratory. Everything said or done to you is a cue; many of them are repeatedly reinforced. This directly contradicts Freudian theory because it claims that nothing is predetermined—there is no id, no instinct, no insight—just learned, conditioned behaviors. Like the old debate about heredity vs. environment, the roots of this conflict go deep in history. John Locke (1632–1704) described the mind as a **tabula rasa** (blank slate), that at birth there is nothing in the mind. "There is nothing in the mind but mind itself," Gottfried von Leibnitz (1646–1716) maintained. He described the mind as a **monad,** a unit of spiritual force, joined to a hierarchy of monads which exist throughout the universe. Behaviorists have produced more research than psychoanalysis or humanistic psychology combined and they are the majority voice in current psychology. Psycho-analysis is the major voice in psychiatry.

HUMANISTIC THEORY

Carl Rogers 1902–1987; Abraham Maslow (1908–1970)

Humanistic theory is a reaction to both psychoanalystic and behavioristic theories. The humanists had no place to go. They were confronted with the "doom and gloom" of Freudian theory with its primitive instincts, incest and death wishes, and the coldly impersonal behaviorists with their rat-maze laboratory approach. They disagreed with both. Two major humanistic theorists emerged, Rogers and Maslow, and while today there are hundreds of variations their basic approach to the nature of personality is still timely and valid.

Rogers' **self theory** emphasized **freedom** (not conformity) as an ongoing process of personal growth and **existence** (existentialism), a focus on the here and now, not the there and then of psychoanalytic or behavioristic theories. He was basic motivation as a movement toward **self actualization.** The best way to do this is to satisfy current needs and to be open and receptive to whatever happens. The **self,** not the libido, is the major personality dynamic. It begins with personal awareness, when you realize the "me" from the "not me" in yourself and by comparing with others. Rogers is remembered also for his concept of **unconditional positive regard** for yourself and others, a powerful supportive measure.

Maslow was originally a behaviorist who became a leading promoter of humanistic theory. We studied his needs levels in Chapter 1. Like Rogers, he saw **self actualization** as life's basic motivation and personality as an ongoing personal growth process throughout life, not a fixed state. He researched this idea and described 15 **B-level characteristics** of self-actualized people, such as being alone but not feeling lonely, independent judgment, individual values and lifestyle, a sense of humor, originality, and creativity. They are **ego transcending** because they go off on their own despite obstacles and what others think and do. They share **B-values** such as: spontaneity; simplicity; honesty; a sense of unity with destiny or fate; the ability to let go of ideas, things and people; childlike playfulness; a feel for beauty and elegance; uniqueness; honesty; and autonomy. Self-actualized people have **peak experiences** usually preceded by wonder, awe, reverence, humility, and surrender. The humanists continue in the spirit and tradition of Leibnitz, the behaviorists to Locke, and the psychoanalysts to Freud.

EXERCISE 6

Read again the three major personality theories. Which is your favorite? Why? What is it in your own personality that led you to that choice? Which do you most dislike? Why? Your choices and opinions can help you understand yourself, to see inside your own personality. To be an expert interviewer or interrogator you must approach everyone you question **without** the bias of any personality theory. As Dr. Kanner, the eminent child psychiatrist said: "The big problem I have with psychoanalytic theory is that the children I talk to haven't read Freud."

SO WHAT?

Why is it necessary to know something about personality theory to interview and interrogate? Because personality **is** human nature and you **must** have a thorough knowledge of it to be able to see what is real and what is a "false front" in people. The vast majority of people are not consciously aware of WHO they are and in most conversations HOW they come across, WHAT or WHY they are. The Scottish poet, Robert Burns (1729–1797), summed up the need to know ourselves and others: "Oh, would some Power the gift to give us, to see ourselves as others see us, would from many a blunder free us." Knowing and using personality theory helps "zero in" on what is said and why it is being said, the personality of the persons behind the conversation. **That** is good interviewing and interrogation.

If Chapter 1 opened you to self-analysis, you should have seen yourself in all three personality theories. As Freud observed, each of us pass through life stages. The id still loves ice cream and doing naughty things from time to time, if the ego can keep superego's heavy hand from punishing us too much with worry and guilt. Every baby is oral then anal, finally genital. Dreams make little sense without Freud's help in seeing into that submerged part of the mind, the unconscious. Freud was right. Everything the behaviorists saw is also right. Like the rifle barrel effect we discussed in Chapter 1. Every mark and scratch we pick up passing through the barrel of life has an effect on us, marks us, shapes our personality. That is learning and conditioning. But there is charm, quiet dignity, a little mystery and magic to personality. That's what makes romance and love possible. Try explaining these qualities by Freudian or behaviorist theories and you may lose your breakfast! If it were left to Freud, having sex would be sufficient. If left to behaviorists, pursuing pleasure would be enough. Humanists add "warm fuzzy" factors to the behaviorists' "cold pricklies" and the Freudians "hot flashes" and sudden impulses. Freud drew a blueprint, behaviorists describe the materials, but humanists tell us we can follow or change the plans and hire and fire the builders of our house of personality.

Freudian theory teaches us we're not so special after all but driven by an instinct-impulse motor roaring inside us with the id at the wheel. There is a lot of animal in us. If you doubt it take a good look at the latest world news. Where do war, crime, and selfishness come from? Freud tells us we are what we feel, where passion leads us. Behaviorist theory teaches us what happens to us makes us special, the result of everything ever said or done to us, like the fingers and hands of an artist shaping clay into an image—personality. Behaviorists tell us we are what has been rewarded and reinforced in us since birth. Humanist theory teaches us that despite Freudian pessimism and behaviorist skepticism we are special just by being human. The world's great art, literature, music and architecture were not created just to vent impulse and instinct as Freud would have it, nor because the creators got pleasure from it, but also and maybe just because of the need to create beauty and elegance, to leave the world better than we found it, to do "the God thing." So what? All personality theories, the "big three" described here and all the others past, present and future, are true because they explain and describe human nature as it is. They describe who, what, why and how we are better than you or I can and that's why they are important. They save us time and help us see with the Zen third eye and hear with the third ear.

EXERCISE 7

Which personality theory do you prefer? Which do you dislike most? Why? Your answers will help you better understand yourself, your attitudes and values, your bias, and personal preferences. How would you improve these theories? Your answer is a test of your wisdom and insight. If this book is used in class as a textbook, discuss this exercise in small groups and then with the whole class.

LEFT BRAIN, RIGHT BRAIN

Carl G. Jung (1875–1961), a psychiatrist who studied with Freud but later struck out on his own to found Analytical Psychology, described people as **introverts** if they preferred to be alone much of the time, or **extroverts** if they generally preferred being with and sharing with others. We know now that most of us are **ambiverts**. There are times we like to be with people and times when we prefer to be alone. It varies with time, place, the other person, our motivation, attitude, and feelings, and opportunity. As with all mental functions, it isn't so simple.

In recent years, there has been increasing interest in brain function. It is now theorized that the left side or left hemisphere in most people is involved with speech, memory, logic, and calculation. The right side or right hemisphere is more involved in abstract ideas, visualizing or conceptualizing, touch, and sensuality. You're really a Dr. Jekyll in the left brain, and Mr. Hyde in the right brain. Left-brained people are into details and make good accountants, bankers, engineers, scientists, mathematicians, technicians, and stock clerks. Right-brained people are into ideas and visualizing things and make good artists, musicians, composers, inventors, designers, fiction writers, poets, philosophers, and clergy. Here's a further comparison:

LEFT BRAIN	RIGHT BRAIN
Facts, details	Ideas, concepts
Organized, structured	Loose, free flowing
Constructive	Creative
Memory files	Here and now experiences
Thinking	Feeling
Logical, analytical	Sensual
Speech	Visual
Digital	Tactile (touch)
"Splitters"	"Lumpers"
Specialists	Generalists

Just as in the case of introverts, extroverts, and amviverts, it appears that most of us are **bilateral**—we use both left and right sides of our brains, though some tend to use one side more than the other. What do **you** use most of the time?

DEFENSE MECHANISMS

We all have and use defense mechanisms. They are verbal and mental evasive techniques used in everyday life to fend off stress, avoid painful realities, and relieve tension. We are like boxers in the ring constantly moving with guard up to avoid getting hit by reality. The Russian mystic Gurdjieff taught that most people behave as if they were asleep and they do not like to be awakened. Your questioning, if effective, will wake up people. They will then react defensively, using one or more **defense mechanisms**. Here's an alphabetical listing:

ACTING OUT. Spontaneous, uncontrolled outburst with no regard for consequences (quick relief of tension); outward expression of an unconscious impulse or wish; it vents feelings explosively so you don't have to consciously wrestle with them; can also be omitting appropriate behavior; the victim can be a person, object or even one's self but more often authority figures, parents, brothers or sisters, friends, children, spouses, or lovers. Examples: Throwing things, self-mutilation, aggravated assault, overeating, smoking when you know its risk.

AFFILIATION. This is the personal and emotional support one gets by joining with others, a fellow feeling of mutual support, persons to confide in who can provide help and advice. It need not involve avoiding personal responsibility, dependency, or manipulating or coercing others to help. Example: Alcoholics Anonymous; church and fraternal organizations; PTA; Boy or Girl Scouts; neighborhood improvement associations; cults; gangs; criminal syndicates.

ALTRUISM. **Altruistic surrender** is doing for others to avoid processing or coping with troubling motives, impulses, thoughts or feelings as if to say: "See, I do good so I must **be** good"; an overcooperative person being interviewed or interrogated may use this defense as a smoke screen. Example: Molly Brown "takes over" and reassures frightened women and children on the deck of the Titanic to see they climb safely and quickly into the lifeboats.

ASCETISM. Rigid self-discipline not allowing any pleasure considered wrong; avoiding conscious, willful pleasure; usually childish nonsense is allowed because it's safe; these **really** uptight people feel good about their self control. Examples: social, political, and religious extremists. A man goes out of his way to avoid even walking on the same street where there are adult sex shops, R or X movies, and avoids magazine and newspaper ads of women's fashions because they may show usually covered parts of the body. He catches the next bus if there are too many women on it. He lives alone, doesn't date, spends his time hermit-like with solitary hobbies.

BLOCKING. Sudden, temporary blocking of a thought or feeling, sometimes in mid-sentence as if insulated from reality or a plug was pulled; the defender can be aware of the blockage and show embarrassment about it. This points up the need to be alert and observant when questioning others so that if blocking occurs you can detect the cause which is likely to be a rich mine of information guarded by such a powerful and dramatic defense.

COMPENSATION. Behavior as if to make up for a real or imagined deficiency or defect. Example: Napoleon's impertinence and audacity on the battlefield as a compensation for his shortness. Some behavioral scientists feel short people tend to be overly assertive. This defense was first described by Dr. Alfred Adler, one of Freud's "inner circle," an opthalmologist by training who observed how one eye will compensate for the weaker eye.

CONTROLLING. Really **overcontrol** of thoughts and feelings, to prevent "going to pieces." Such persons appear robot-like, very mechanical and without emotion, as if in a daze. Could be drug-induced.

DELUSION. Fixed false belief changing the real to the unreal, usually with either a grandiose or a paranoid (persecuted) theme. This is usually a symptom of severe mental disorder. Examples: "The devil is tearing my guts up" (psychotic depression); "The FBI sends messages to the radio implanted in my brain" (schizophrenia); "I killed him because he was going to steal my brain" (paranoid psychosis). Key factor: delusions are **not** based at all on reality, as in the joke: "You ain't paranoid if they're **really** out to get you!" **Projection, isolation,** and **introjection** may contain peculiar ideas, but they are **always** based on reality, even if exaggerated.

DENIAL–AVOIDANCE (sometimes considered separate defenses). **Denial** is an automatic disconnect to disturbing realities; such persons keep missing the point when most people would not. **Avoidance** is more subtle, less direct and dramatic, more evasive such as pretending not to see or hear what is uncomfortable, not commenting on it, quickly ending the conversation, or changing the subject. Denial and avoidance are frequently seen in interview and interrogation and you need to develop your observational skills to quickly detect them. Examples: "I don't have AIDS even though the lab tests are positive — they're not always accurate." "This hacking cough has nothing to do with my smoking two packs a day." Involved in a difference of opinion which becomes more heated, a friend interrupts to observe that you're getting upset and you snap back: "Upset? Who the hell's upset?" Left alone at home with a full cookie jar, empty when Mommy returns, little Amy, confronted with the evidence says: "I didn't eat'em" (**denial**). "You probably forgot to fill the jar" (**rationalization**). A crime suspect, caught in the act, sits calmly when charged and shrugs his shoulders saying nothing and showing no emotion.

DEVALUATION (discounting, minimization). Magnified, exaggerated negative aspects of one's self or others, described in critical, sarcastic terms or with cutting humor.

DISPLACEMENT (stereotyping, scapegoating). Attention or blame focussed on weaker persons, animals, or some object; the emotions most often involved are sexual (child molesting or sexual abuse) or anger such as in this example: the boss dumps on you; you can't tell him off so you take it home and dump on your wife. She won't give it back to you so she dumps on an older kid who dumps on a younger kid who kicks the dog who in a frenzy chases the cat who kills more mice than his quota. The Mice Federation meets, confused and upset about the rising mouse murder rate. Displacement can also be kicking a flat tire in frustration, throwing a hammer that missed a nail and dented the wall, or shooting highway signs in hunting season when no game appeared that day.

DISSOCIATION. Drastic change of personality or identity or temporary amnesia, fugue state, or conversion reaction triggered like a circuit breaker cutting off wiring to memory, identity, and thinking; can also be an outburst of reckless abandon or sudden overactivity but of shorter duration than **acting-out**. Examples: the movies *Sybil* and *Three Faces of Eve*, police officer's trigger finger paralyzed after shooting someone (medically impossible); "glove" paralysis of a hit-

and-run driver's hands after running someone down (also medically impossible).

DISTORTION. Gross reframing or reshaping of reality to better fit your own needs and to make painful reality more easily tolerated. Example: Hit by a car, Bea Goode is dying and knows it. Asked if she wants family notified she smiles saying: "Well, my husband is out of the country away on business, and I don't know how to reach him. I'm sure he'd want to know," Just saying this comforts her. Actually, she has no husband and no immediate family.

FANTASY. It is **autistic** if it is daydreaming which substitutes for everyday behaviors, dreamlike behavior at work, home, or in relationships. It is **schizoid** if it is an escape into thoughts and feelings of unreality and results in eccentric behavior to keep others at a safe distance. Fantasy-like behaviors can also be drug-induced. Examples: Mary had a miscarriage, her first pregnancy. She walked down the hospital corridor, looking in at the babies and, humming a lullaby, deciding what she would name each if they were her own.

HUMOR. To emphasize humor or irony to avoid painful reality and without offending others. Healthy humor enables you to process painful reality but at the same time laugh at it, rendering it less painful. Example: An older woman, raped, comments with a weak smile that she's old enough to be the rapist's mother. A police officer who with one shot killed an armed bank robber says: "I barely qualified this year yet I killed him with one shot."

IDEALIZATION. Exaggerated positive qualities of one's self or others. Examples: A person who has lived in a foreign country or a distant big city goes to great length to boast about how everything about it is "great." A graduate of a certain university, former FBI or CIA agent describe at length how superior are those organizations. See also **affiliation**.

INHIBITION. Limiting of personality function, thoughts or feelings as if to "go dead" or "freeze up."

INTELLECTUALIZATION. Reciting about, not realizing what's happening; thinking not feeling or doing; overthinking or "head tripping"; trying to use "super logic" or "word magic" to make what's real unreal, abstract, mysterious, foggy—and safe—a "verbal snake bite kit." Differs from **rationalization** by its motive which is to shield or protect the self against painful realities. You don't have to be intelligent to intellectualize—they're not the same.

INTROJECTION. "Swallowing the monster," taking upon one's self qualities of others, to feel close to them or, if involving someone feared, to neutralize threat and control the aggressor.

ISOLATION. Words without feeling; the emotions not allowed into consciousness thus not into the conversation; splitting emotion from thinking or the memory of an event; can also switch to a different, safer, less painful thought or emotion similar to **displacement**. Example: Badly injured crime victim describes minute details of the attack totally without emotion.

PASSIVE–AGGRESSION. Disguised, indirect way of expressing hostility to others through passivity, such as delay, illness, incomplete tasks, and in interviewing incomplete answers, inattention, seeming not to hear or understand, acting silly or asking for a drink of water or cigarette. Example: A rookie at the pistol range missed the target. The range officer hands him a box of bullets and says: "It's OK. Take your time. I got all day and a hundred more boxes here."

PROJECTION (externalization). Falsely blaming or seeing in others your own real motives, impulses, thoughts or feelings; the unconscious rejection of disturbing motives, impulses, thoughts or feelings, externalizing them to someone or something else. Examples: Jealousy; racial prejudice; vigilantes; political or nationalist extremism (terrorism); religious bigotry; inciting a riot; "witch hunt" or "lynch mob" behavior (group hysteria).

RATIONALIZATION. Making excuses; inventing incorrect but reassuring explanations; over-justification; playing the "yes, but" game. Example: "I've heard many excuses but not one good reason" (Robert Louis Stevenson). Rationalization is **not** lying. Lying is conscious; rationalization is unconscious in the Freudian sense. Differs from **intellectualization** by its motive which is self-justification.

REACTION FORMATION. Saying or doing the opposite to how you really feel or strikingly different than one would reasonably expect to react. Example: You really like someone but are aloof and treat him or her with indifference because you're afraid to show your true feelings. You go out of your way to be nice to someone you despise "killing them with kindness." Pretty Pat, recovering from a hysterectomy, tells husband: "Well, this will be a great relief. No more worry about getting pregnant, taking the pills, nine months of discomfort, the pain of childbirth, the time and money and worry of kids." She smiles saying this but holds his hand tightly and there are tears in her eyes.

REGRESSION. Returning (regressing) to previous ways of coping with stress (running away and hiding, sitting alone with lights out, fleeing to bed, temper tantrums, hysterical weeping or laughter) or to a previous stage (acting childish). Examples: "Baby talk," playful kidding or teasing, the childish behaviors of lovers, party behavior (birthday parties, New Year's Eve, Mardi Gras, Halloween).

REPRESSION. Expelling from your mind disturbing motives, impulses, thoughts, feelings, or painful memories as if "kicking them downstairs" below consciousness (the Freudian unconscious); resembles a memory lapse, an unusual "mental block," and often the person repressing shows symbolic behavior which s/he cannot explain and which can be upsetting (Gregory Peck in *Spellbound*). Repression is unintentional, automatic, unconscious. Differs from **suppression** because the person is not consciously aware. Example: A woman raped in a red van cannot consciously remember the vehicle but has panic attacks whenever she sees a van and is upset by the color red. A man weeps as you question him though the questions are routine and involve no emotional content. He cannot explain why he weeps. There is a definite reason for these behaviors, but neither the woman nor the man know what it is. Told she can never have children, the newly married woman adjusts to this reality, but when invited to a Christmas party she is upset and weeps, not knowing why. Clue: Christmas is somebody's **birthday** and Christmas cards are full of baby pictures!

SEXUALIZATION. Attaching sexual significance to a person or object which a reasonable person would not identify as sexual, to avoid sexual impulses yourself. Example: You control your sexual impulses but get "turned on" driving through a tunnel or plugging in an appliance (they symbolize the sex act; electrical plugs are sometimes called the "male plug").

SOMATIZATION. Converting psychological-emotional problems into somatic symptoms (psychosomatic) so as to be preoccupied with physical symptoms or body function to an exaggerated extent. Examples of mind-body connections: You get a headache or your stomach churns whenever the boss is near. You make sexual overtures and are told: "I really do have a headache." Listen for mind-body references in daily conversation, such as "he broke my heart . . . she's a pain in the neck . . . I busted my ass for you . . . they had me by the short and curlies." Hypochondriacs complain to get attention, punish, control, or manipulate those who care for/about them.

SPLITTING. All-or-nothing perception of self or others seen as opposites, all good or all evil with no middle ground because the individual can't cope with or reconcile contradictory attitudes, thoughts, or feelings about self or others. Examples: Asked why the job applicant left the last job s/he replies: "They were all screwed up." This person can't cope with firms or people being a mixture of good and bad.

SUBLIMATION. Channeling disturbing urges and impulses into socially acceptable behaviors. Examples: A child molester attempts to join Big Brothers. A gay woman applies to a women's gym as massage therapist. Contact sports or artistic expression—but only to defend against external or internal stress or conflict. Example: It's Friday night and Fast Freddy calls on Cool Kate. He hugs her and she says: "Oh, there's a party at Grizelda Ghoul's, let's go." At the party Freddy holds her close, breathing heavily, but Kate says: "Let's dance." After many dances, on the way home, Freddy parks at a moonlit lake and kisses Kate who says: "Race you to the barn." Kate is trying to **sublimate** Freddy's sex drive.

SUPPRESSION. Intentional conscious or partially conscious postponing dealing with disturbing motives, impulses, thoughts, feelings, or painful memories. Example: A child abused by a grandparent makes excuses so as not to be near the grandparent and avoids neighbors who are of the same age. Suppressed material can be recalled, sometimes with effort. It differs from **repression** and **denial** in the common motive to **permanently** prevent recall and from **rationalization** which is evasive.

SYMBOLIZATION. Really a form of repression, where a person or object represents someone or something else which caused psychological pain. Examples: Rapists who symbolize women as mother figures or women who have mistreated them; thieves who rob to take back from "the rich" what they feel they are entitled; the "cop killer" sees law enforcement officers as symbolic substitutes for his father who physically and verbally abused him.

UNDOING. To make up for negative thoughts, feelings or actions; first **doing** something negative, causing anxiety or guilt then **undoing** it with opposite positive behavior, reparation, or apology. This defense confuses victims because one never knows what the real feelings are, what was first vented (doing) or the followup (undoing). Example: In a rage, Mary breaks a dish over John's head, then within seconds tearfully apologizes, gently putting a bandage on the cut.

There can be overlap of these defense mechanisms and some are inter-related. For example, intellectualization shares features of isolation, rationalization, sublimation, and undoing. Acting out, dissociation, and distortion share certain features as do altruism, sublimation, and displacement. The defense mechanisms, their definitions, and the examples given are very important to a better understanding of human nature and the workings of the mind. You will see every one of these defenses the longer you question people. By knowing them **now** you will be able to more quickly see through them to more effectively get at the truth. The **scientific** interviewer-interrogator is forewarned and forearmed with this indepth knowledge of behavior. Defense mechanisms are part of normal behavior, but in disturbed people they can be exaggerated and therefore abnormal.

EXERCISE 8

Review the defense mechanisms. Identify those that you yourself use. Write them down. You will spot them in others quickly, since you use them yourself. Focus on those you **don't** use and study them so that you won't miss them when you see them.

Your Four Selves

Karen Horney (1885–1952), a psychiatrist and psychoanalyst, described the self concept as composed of four different types:

PERSONAL SELF: This is the person you think you are. At times, you yourself don't know what and why you think and feel as you do, so the **personal self** is not 100 percent you.

IDEALIZED SELF: The person you'd really like to be. Freudians say you'll never make it, your id will trip you. Humanists say you never stop growing. Behaviorists say tomorrow there'll be another set of cues on the rat-maze of life. The idealized you is somewhere in the future, not here today.

REPUTATIONAL SELF: The person others think you are. This is the person described in letters, diaries, conversations, phone calls, impressions and, opinions of others. It's all in sound, on paper, not you.

REAL SELF: The real, authentic you, in the flesh, as you **really** are, despite what others see, probably despite what you see (is your lens clean?).

Expert interviewers and interrogators can differentiate all four of these self concepts and focus on the most important—the real self. None of the others are real. None of the others are there, they don't exist. Only one is **scientifically** valid—that person, that personality, will soon be sitting right there, waiting for your next question to tease out the **real self.**

EXERCISE 9

Using Horney's four selves, reflect on how you would be described according to each. Imagine how the kind of person you typically interview or interrogate would compare. Same? Different? Why?

WHAT'S ABNORMAL?

This chapter began with a description of "normal" or "healthy" personality development. For most of us, what was described there is what happens to us despite life's setbacks and stresses. We turn now from the "normal" to the "abnormal," from mental health to mental illness. Karen Horney described ten **neurotic needs** which can lead to serious social and psychological problems. Today the term **disorder** is used to describe abnormal behaviors and **neurosis** is fading from use. Still, Dr. Horney's list is helpful in explaining what motivates some people.

1. EXCESS AFFECTION OR APPROVAL. We all need a certain amount of affection and approval, but when this need becomes

neurotic, sick, it leads to a never-ending, desperate search such as frequent job changes, divorce, moving, or becoming increasingly irritable, blaming, demanding, or manipulative.

2. PARTNER TO TAKE OVER. Some women seek a Sir Galahad to sweep them off their feet to a castle in the sky where there are no bills or problems. Some men seek a "big Momma" to hold them close, make everything right, and kiss the boo-boos away. Doing so can make you totally dependent on a person who also has problems and rob both of you of dignity and individuality.

3. NARROW LIMITS. When you pull back, lower your sights, you structure everything so that its predictable and safe. It can be tiring and stressful taking on too much and people who narrow their limits prefer to underdo than to do or overdo.

4. POWER. These are the overly ambitious who ruthlessly use others in their quest for power. To them people are mere pawns on the chessboard of life. Their goal is power, as much as they can get, without limit, at any price.

5. PRESTIGE. Those who cannot have direct power and control settle for the next best thing, prestige. When others defer to them as special, give them status, it sets them off as important, better— a form of power.

6. EXPLOITATION. These are the opportunists, clever manipulators. They enjoy the game of "pulling strings" more than the power or prestige payoffs described above. They move in on any situation they feel they can turn to their advantage.

7. PERSONAL ADMIRATION. These are the "ego trippers" who want to be famous, admired, idolized. They usually "dress up" and make a special effort to look good, say and do just the right thing, as if waiting for the cameras and reporters, which never come.

8. ACHIEVEMENT. These appear to be "workaholics," but their extra effort is not to help an organization or to make a contribution, but to win victories in an endless series of battles, unable to take time to relax and enjoy success, but moving on to the next engagement.

9. SELF–SUFFICIENCY. These people expend extra effort to make sure they don't owe anybody anything, to be absolutely and totally independent. They do fall in love but are really incapable of establishing and maintaining a lasting, intimate relationship with anyone.

10. PERFECTION. To be perfect is to be invulnerable. No one hurt

you. You are on the high ground, holding the castle. Being perfect is to have few if any equals, so there is no need to spoil one's self by mixing with dummies like you and me.

MENTAL DISORDERS

The standard reference for classifying and describing mental disorders is the latest edition of the *Diagnostic and Statistical Manual of Mental Disorders*, known as "the DSM" and published about every ten years by the American Psychiatric Association. What follows is based on the DSM–III–R (1987), a revision of the 1980 DSM–III, which will be the standard until 1992 when DSM–IV is released. But first a word of caution! Alexander Pope wrote in 1722: "A little bit of learning is a dangerous thing; drink deep or taste not . . . " Mastering the information in these pages does not qualify you to diagnose mental illness or to analyze personalities. It is provided to deepen your understanding of how people think, what they feel, why they behave as they do, so that you can separate fact from fiction in your questioning.

In case you haven't by now reached a conclusion, human behavior is very complex. The mind is more complicated than a computer. The DSM contains hundreds of specialized terms, each involving concepts that would take several volumes to describe. Still, it is important that you understand how a mind strays from normal to abnormal. The longer you are in contact with people, especially interviewing or interrogating, the more likely you are to see abnormal behavior. I have arranged DSM diagnoses for easier teaching and learning. There are additional recommended readings listed at the end of this chapter if you would like to learn more about mental disorders or build a useful reference library.

ORGANIC OR FUNCTIONAL?

The first "cut" or sorting out of mental disorders is to separate the **organic** from **functional** disorders.

ORGANIC MENTAL DISORDERS are due to brain damage (like "being wired wrong") or brain dysfunction (a malfunction). Organic mental disorders have a variety of causes: a stroke, penetrating wounds, fractured skull, closed head injury, tumors, infection, severe nutritional deficiencies, toxic substances, substance abuse, or senility. The most common types of organic mental disorders are:

Delirium
Dementia
Amnestic disorder
Organic delusional disorder
Organic hallucinosis
Organic mood disorder
Organic anxiety disorder
Organic personality disorder

Delirium. Consciousness (awake, alert, attentive) comes and goes unpredictably like sun and shade on a cloudy day, or a light bulb that randomly dims and brightens. These persons will answer a question the same as the previous question or ramble and overanswer, go off on a tangent, or mumble incoherently. Questions must be repeated and in simple language. There is difficulty with two or more of these: may look sleepy; respond slowly with many pauses; frequently misunderstand you; doesn't know the day, date, place, or time; can't remember past events or what was asked and discussed before; hallucinates (sees or hears what isn't there).

Dementia. Consciousness is clear (definition above) and they are oriented (know who and where they are) but have poor short-term memory (recent events, new information today, this week) and long-term memory (remote or past events, life and work history) and difficulty with one or more of these: can't abstract (understand proverbs or sayings, define words or concepts, see similarities); poor judgment in social, family, or job settings; recognize but can't name things, do simple tasks or draw three-dimensional figures; change in personality (exaggerated or different).

Amnestic Disorder (amnestic is the new term for **amnesia**). Consciousness and abstraction (defined above) are intact but memory, especially for recent events, is impaired.

Organic Delusional Disorder. Delusions caused **only** by a physical or external factor such as temporal lobe epilepsy or drugs, especially amphetamines, cocaine, steroids, bromocriptine (Parlodel), indomethacin (Indocin), or propanolol (Inderal). **Delusions** are clearly false, unreal beliefs, usually with peculiar dreamlike content and one of two themes: **grandiosity** or greatness ("I am God") to the opposite, being persecuted ("The Martians are going to kill me!"). Delusions also occur in **psychosis** described later in this chapter.

Organic Hallucinosis. Hallucinations, seeing, or hearing what are not there, not real, caused **only** physical or organic factors such as sensory deprivation (severe social isolation can do it), hallucinogenic drugs, amphetamines and stimulants, anticonvulsants, steroids, digitalis (Crystodigin and others), levodopa or L-dopa (Larodopa, Sinemet) or ketamine (Ketaject, Ketalar). Hallucinations are very common in **schizophrenia** described later in this chapter.

Organic Mood Disorder. Manic, depressive or mixed manic and depressive disorder caused **only** by organic factors, usually drugs (certain prescribed medications, alcohol, and street drugs) or physical illness.

Organic Anxiety Disorder. Panic attacks and very high anxiety caused **only** by organic factors such as rebound effect from alcohol or drug withdrawal. You may have had a small sample of this one if you've tried to stop smoking.

Organic Personality Disorder is a personality change which persists (not due to a temporary stress situation), either an exaggeration of the old personality or markedly different, caused **only** by organic factors such as brain damage or temporal lobe epilepsy with one or more of these: marked changes of mood (normal to anxiety, depression, or anger); repeated angry outbursts far out of proportion to the cause; poor social judgment (often sexual); suspicious of others (paranoid); marked apathy and indifference. Called **explosive type** if rage outbursts predominate.

Also listed under organic mental disorders are **intoxication, withdrawal** (if relevant), **dependence,** and **abuse,** for alcohol, amphetamines, caffeine (coffee), cannabis (marihuana), cocaine, hallucinogens, inhalants, opoids, PCP, sedatives, hypnotics (sleeping pills), anxiolytics (tranquilizers) and "other unspecified psychoactive (mind altering) substances." **Mental retardation** is NOT listed as an organic disorder but as a **developmental disorder** with autism, academic, language, and speech, and motor skills disorders. Consult the recommended readings listed at the end of this chapter if you want further details about these substance abuse and developmental disorders.

FUNCTIONAL DISORDERS

When mental disorders have no physical, organic cause they are said to be **functional disorders.** For ease of teaching and learning they are divided into three categories: **psychosis; personality disorders; "reactive disorders."** Psychosis is more severe than personality or reactive disorders, so disruptive it prevents living a normal, productive life or even surviving if left alone, and satisfies legal criteria for involuntary commitment: mentally ill, a danger to self or others, unable to care for self and in need of treatment. **Personality disorders** are lifelong established patterns of behavior, recognizable from childhood to the present. **Reactive disorders** is not an official DSM term but is used in this book to more easily compare and differentiate them from other disorders.

Psychosis

There are two major types of psychosis: **thought disorders** which distort thinking and ideas of reality (schizophrenia, paranoia) and **mood disorders** which disturb emotions and feelings (bipolar affective disorder, new name for manic-depressive, and major depression). Here's how DSM lists them:

Schizophrenia
    Catatonic, disorganized, paranoid, residual, or undifferentiated
Delusional (paranoid) disorder
    Erotomanic, grandiose, jealous, persecutory, or somatic
Mood disorders
    Bipolar disorder (mixed, manic, or depressed), Cyclothymia
Depressive disorders
    Major depression (single episode or recurrent) Dysthymia
Psychoses not elsewhere classified
    Brief reactive psychosis, schizophreniform, schizoaffective, induced psychotic disorders

Schizophrenia

Schizophrenia is a psychotic thought disorder with these disturbed thoughts and impaired behaviors for more than six months: bizarre delusions (often about thought broadcasting, control, or implantation); hallucinations (usually blaming, critical or commanding voices); deterioration on the job and socially, and two or more of these: delusions (grandiose or persecuting); prominent, persistent hallucinations (at least several times a week for more than a few minutes); loose associations (incorrect, illogical, or bizarre connections between ideas; nonsense words; jumbled "word salad"); flat (emotionless) or inappropriate affect (giggling, laughing for no reason); lack of insight (awareness of reality, understanding what is happening. There are several types of schizophrenia:
    Catatonic if there is one or more of these: mutism or catatonic stupor

(motionless, speechless, staring); catatonic rigidity (statue-like holding a rigid posture even when moved); catatonic posturing (voluntary rigid pose, like a patient at the VA Hospital standing at attention all day); catatonic negativism (opposing all requests and actions without reason).

Disorganized. Loose associations, flat or inappropriate affect, and grossly disorganized behavior which is erratic, inconsistent, futile, as if thinking is fragmented.

Paranoid. Major obvious symptom is deeply entrenched delusions and/or frequent auditory hallucinations and with **no** loose associations, flat or inappropriate affect, catatonic or disorganized behavior.

Residual. No delusions, hallucinations, incoherence or grossly disorganized behaviors but two or more of these: social isolation; impaired function at job, school or work; lack of initiative; peculiar behavior; odd beliefs or magical thinking; unusual perception (like sensing someone's presence who's not there); poor grooming or hygiene; blunted or inappropriate affect; impaired speech (vague, sparse, overdone).

Undifferentiated. Delusions, hallucinations, incoherence or grossly disorganized behaviors, a smorgasbord of schizophrenic symptoms.

Delusional (Paranoid) Disorders

These are delusions embedded in everyday life situations a month or more which do not appear as bizarre as those seen in schizophrenia. Hallucinations are rare and behavior is otherwise normal. The delusion itself is abnormal and they are named by type: **erotomanic,** that someone usually of higher status is in love with you; **grandiose,** that you are a special person; **jealous,** that your spouse or lover is unfaithful; **persecutory,** that you or a loved one is being victimized; **somatic,** a firm belief something is wrong with you.

Mood Disorders

Mood Disorders divide into bipolar disorders (mixed, manic or depressed, and cyclothymia) and depressive disorders (major depression and dysthymia):

Bipolar Disorder, Mixed. Abnormally high, elevated mood (mania) with three or more of these: inflated self-esteem and grandiosity; decreased need for sleep; excessively talkative (pressured speech); racing thoughts (flight of ideas); easily distracted (sensitive to external cues); self-indulgence (buying sprees, binges); unrealistic goals. Also gets depressed, but duration is no more than two weeks.

Bipolar Disorder, Manic. Mania only, no depression. Can be seasonal.

Bipolar Disorder, Depressed. Has had one or more manic episodes but is now depressed.

Cyclothymia. For two years or more there have been mood swings up and down but not as marked or severe as bipolar disorder.

Depressive Disorders are classified as single episode or recurrent, occur in persons who have never had a manic episode, and who have five or more of these nearly every day: depressed most of the time; lack of interest in pleasurable activities most of the time; more than 5 percent weight gain or loss per month; insomnia or oversleeping; over- or under-activity as noticed by others; fatigue or loss of energy; feeling guilty or worthless; poor concentration; recurring thoughts of death or suicide (not grieving over actual death of someone). **Single episode** is a continuing depression, **recurrent** is a major depression which returns despite periods of normal mood. Major depression can be seasonal. **Dysthymia** (formerly depressive neurosis) is depressed mood most of the time on most days for more than two months at a time for two years or more and with two or more of these: poor appetite or overeating; insomnia or oversleeping; fatigue or lack of energy; low self-esteem; poor concentration, indecisive; feeling hopeless. Dysthymia is **primary** if it exists of and by itself and **secondary** if related or secondary to other disorders.

Psychotic Disorders Not Elsewhere Classified

Brief Reactive Psychosis. Lasts from a few hours to a month with return to normal functioning; rapid changes of intense mood or overwhelming confusion and one or more of these: loose associations or incoherence; delusions; hallucinations; catatonic or disorganized behavior.

Schizophreniform Disorder. Symptoms of schizophrenia but for less than six months.

Schizoaffective Disorder. Combines symptoms of schizophrenia and bipolar disorder or major depression.

Induced psychotic disorder (shared paranoid disorder). A paranoid delusion in a second person induced from close contact with a delusional person; content is similar.

Psychotic Disorder Not Otherwise Specified (NOS), formerly called **atypical psychosis,** includes psychotic disorders which don't meet criteria for other psychoses or where there is insufficient information to make a firm diagnosis. The DSM has such an "NOS" (not otherwise specified) category for each group of disorders.

Personality Disorders

Personality Disorders are established patterns and traits and behaviors of long-standing, usually from childhood or teen years, which interfere with optimal adjustment in social or job settings or cause the person problems. The DSM groups them into three **clusters:**

Cluster A Personality Disorders are those of people who have a peculiar attitude toward others and to life:

Paranoid, with four or more of: expects to be harmed or exploited; suspects others are disloyal or unreliable; suspects spouse/lover is unfaithful; sees hidden meanings in innocent events; bears grudges; won't confide in others; hypersensitive.

Schizoid. Social isolation or withdrawal with four or more of: ambivalent toward family and friends (take it or leave it indifference); no close friends or just one; a loner; low sex drive; doesn't show or seem to have strong emotions; aloof, dull, expressionless face, rarely nods or gestures to others; unmoved by praise or criticism.

Schizotypal. Peculiar ideas (off the wall) and appearance (garish clothes, mismatched colors) with five or more of: ideas of reference (innocent events misinterpreted as personal); very nervous around others; odd beliefs or superstitious or magical thinking; unusual perceptions (someone or something is there); odd behaviors and mannerisms; odd speech (vague, tangential, abstract); no more than one close friend (often none); suspicious of others; inappropriate or constricted affect (silly or aloof).

Cluster B Personality Disorders are those which involve a basic aggressive or manipulative approach to personal and social relationships:

Antisocial. Age 18 or older with a history of antisocial behavior and **before age 15** three or more of: frequent truancy; ran away from home more than twice; started fights; has used a weapon more than once; forced sex on someone; cruel to others; cruel to animals; destroyed property; set fires; often lied; theft or forgery more than once, no physical contact; robbed someone with physical contact or with weapon. **Since age 15** four or more of: absent from work often, unemployed six months or more, impulsive job changes; unlawful behavior; irritable and aggressive (assaults, fights); financially irresponsible; impulsive, a drifter; lies (cons, uses aliases); reckless, endangers others; if a parent, neglects child; can't maintain monogamous relationship for more than a year.

Borderline. Erratic, unstable relationships and self-image with five or more of: extremes of approval and disapproval of self; impulsive (sex, money, substance abuse, driving, binge eating); mood swings; unable to manage strong emotions; suicidal threats or gestures or self-mutilation; identity, sex or role confusion; feels empty and bored; frantic about being abandoned.

Histrionic. Dramatic and attention-seeking with four or more of: constantly seeks reassurance; inappropriately sexually seductive appearance and behavior; overconcerned about attractiveness; exaggerated emotion (gushy, weepy, temper tantrums); uncomfortable if not center of attention; shallow feelings quickly changing; selfish, gotta have it now, can't wait; impressive speech but lacks detail.

Narcissistic. In love with self and quite pleased about it, with five or more of: over-reacting to criticism; exploits others; self-centered, exaggerates achievements; is special, associates only with other special people; daydreams of ideal love, power, wealth; feels entitled to special treatment; wants constant attention; lacks empathy; loaded with envy.

Cluster C Personality Disorders involve underlying fear and insecurity about self and others:

Avoidant. Fear of disapproval with four or more of: feelings easily hurt; one or no close friends; avoids social contact; avoids jobs with people contact; passive around people because afraid to look foolish; afraid of blushing, crying, showing fear; exaggerates risk or dangers.

Dependent, passive and submissive, with five or more of: unable to make decisions; likes others to make decisions; agrees rather than be rejected; avoids independent activities; does dirty jobs to get accepted; doesn't like to be alone; overreacts to end of relationships; fears being abandoned; feelings easily hurt.

Obsessive-Compulsive. Rigid perfectionists and nitpickers, with five or more of: strict personal standards interfere with getting anything done; so far into details can't see the major goal; insist others do the same or they want to do it themselves because no one else can; workaholic to the exclusion of having fun; indecisive, never has enough data; overly high morals and ethics; can't show affection; stingy unless there's a payoff; packrat, won't throw anything out.

Passive-Aggressive. Passive resister, obstructionist foot-dragger, with five or more of: procrastinates; angry, irritated or moody if asked to do something; works slow; resents and protests "unreasonable demands"; conveniently "forgets" obligations; sees self as a good worker though others do not; resents suggestions from others; obstructs others by not being a team player; criticizes those in authority.

Reactive Disorders

These are reactions to sudden or long-term stress. How would you react to unexpected, severe stress? Would you "freak out" and "go bananas," flee or freeze, fight back or fold, get sick or get drunk or high? Reactive disorders are all of these and here's the "Whitman's Sampler" of them: They are named for their major characteristic:

Anxiety disorders   Sexual disorders
Dissociative disorders   Factitious disorders
Somatoform disorders   Sleep disorders
Adjustment disorders   Impulse disorders
            Psychoactive substance use disorders

ANXIETY DISORDERS

These involve excessive fear, uncertainty, apprehension, or threat, narrowly focussed or generalized. They are:

Panic Disorder (Without Agoraphobia) are unexpected panic attacks (periods of intense fear or discomfort) when not the focus of anyone's attention. They only last a few minutes but are terrifying, with one or more of these: shortness of breath or suffocating sensation; chest pain; choking; dizzy or faint; nausea or upset stomach; palpitations or rapid heart; trembling; sweating; depersonalization ("Is this me?") or derealization ("Is this really happening?"); numbness or tingling; chills or hot flashes; fear of dying; fear of going crazy. If they have four or more of these it's a **panic attack**; if fewer it's a **limited symptom attack**.

Panic Disorder With Agoraphobia. Same as above but with additional **extreme** fear of being anywhere you might not escape or be rescued from and going out of your way to avoid such places and situations. Typical terrifying situations: home alone; away from home; in crowds; standing in line; in a shopping mall, theater, or restaurant; on a beach, boat or ship, airliner, train, bus, taxi or car; bridges; tunnels.

Social Phobia. Unrealistic, extreme fear of being criticized, laughed at, embarrassed and humiliated for saying or doing something foolish, choking on food, being unable to talk, unable to go to the bathroom, that you're smelly or you'll tremble and shake, and going out of your way to avoid situations where these may occur even though highly unlikely.

Single Phobia. Unrealistic, extreme fear of a specific object or situation and going out of your way to avoid it. Can involve any of the situations above or anything around you—snakes, spiders, roaches, rats, hospitals, dentists, sex, etc.

Obsessive-Compulsive Disorder. It's **obsessive** if you have recurrent thoughts or ideas (**Is the front door locked? You're gonna get cancer**). It's **compulsive** if you **must** do repetitive, ritualistic acts (**step on every crack on the sidewalk; go try the front door several times, turning the knob many times**). It's a disorder if you spend more than an hour a day with these, it interferes with job or social relations and causes you marked distress.

Posttraumatic Stress Disorder from a severely stressful event (combat, accident, catastrophe, violent crime) which is reexperienced by flashbacks or dreams or fear it's recurring or extreme distress in similar settings or at anniversaries of the event and three or more of these: avoiding thoughts or feelings similar to the event; avoiding anything that would remind you of it; amnesia for some aspect of it; lack of interest in what you used to like to do; feeling detached from others; unable to love, care; sense of impending doom, untimely end, and two or more of these: insomnia; awakening; irritable with angry outbursts; can't concentrate; overly vigilant; jumpy; physical reaction to similar setting (rapid heart or sweating or hyperventilation).

Generalized Anxiety Disorder. Unrealistic, excessive anxiety and worry on most days and for six months or more, about two or more life situations (finances, children, marriage, job, etc.) with six or more of these: trembling; sore or tight muscles; restless; tires easily; shortness of breath or suffocating sensation; palpitations or rapid heart; sweating or clammy hands; dry mouth; dizzy; nausea, diarrhea, or upset stomach; chills or hot flashes; frequent urination; lump in throat; edgy; jumpy; can't concentrate; insomnia, awakens; irritable.

DISSOCIATIVE DISORDERS are dramatic changes in personality function (consciousness, perception of reality, identity, memory):

Multiple Personality Disorder or "split personality," when there are two or more distinct personal identities in one individual, each of which can at times take over complete control. This is usually a reaction to extreme cruelty in childhood when there is no escape except by becoming someone else. To see movie versions of this, *Three Faces of Eve* and *Sybil* are available on videotape.

Psychogenic Fugue is assuming a different identity partially or fully and being unable to recall the past; usually occurs with unexpected travel away from home or work.

Psychogenic Amnesia is a sudden inability to know or remember important personal information such as your name, address, age, occupation, or to recognize family or friends.

Depersonalization Disorder is a trance-like, unreal experience of feeling outside your body or like a robot or in a dream, causing marked distress, but all other reality contact is normal.

Dissociative State Not Otherwise Specified. Dazed "not with it" behavior occurring in some cult members, terrorist captives or prisoners of war, accident or crime victims, recently abused children, or altered states of consciousness (meditation, artistic reverie, religious devotion). Actually, people deeply in love resemble this disorder—Plato said "love is a grave mental disease." Maybe this is it! Also in this category is **Ganser's syndrome** where wrong but weakly related answers are given to direct questions. Examples: How much is 1 + 1? "Three." Who was President during World War II? "Eisenhower."

SOMATOFORM DISORDERS are mind-body reactions and they are:

Body Dysmorphic Disorder, being excessively preoccupied with an imagined defect or an exaggerated real minor defect.

Conversion Disorder, a change or loss of body function which occurs under stress or with strong emotion; it is usually symbolically connected to psychological factors. Examples: Numbing or complete loss of sensation in genitalia after being raped. Trigger finger paralysis after shooting someone.

Hypochondriasis is an exaggerated fear or unfounded conviction for more than six months that you have a disease; can result from misinterpreting symptoms; there is no medical evidence to confirm the feared condition.

Somatization Disorder exists if before age 30 you have a history of physical complaints or believe you are sickly and with 13 or more of these without medical confirmation of an organic cause (the first 7 are most common): vomiting; shortness of breath; amnesia; difficulty swallowing; pain in arms or legs; burning sensation in rectum or genitals; painful menstruation; nausea; stomach pain; bloating; diarrhea; can't tolerate certain foods; palpitations; dizziness; loss of voice; deafness; double vision; blurred vision; blindness; fainting or unconsciousness; seizures; trouble walking; weak or numb muscles; back pain; joint pain; painful urination; difficulty urinating; pain other than headaches; little or no sex drive; painful intercourse; impotence; irregular menstrual periods; excessive menstrual flow; vomiting throughout pregnancy.

Somatoform Pain Disorder is preoccupation with functional pain for more than six months with either no proven organic cause or where pain is grossly excessive according to medical examination and opinion.

Undifferentiated Somatoform Disorder. Physical problems for more than six months either without proven organic cause or which is grossly excessive according to medical examination and opinion.

ADJUSTMENT DISORDERS occur within three months of a stressful event or situation and last up to six months, are not the person's usual reaction and exceed it and what would be expected of a normal, reasonable person, and interfere with everyday living. They are:

Adjustment Disorder With Anxious Mood, where anxiety is the major symptom (Example: Thorndyke, aspiring writer, gets rejection notices every day and is now so nervous and upset he can't write).

Adjustment Disorder With Depressed Mood, where depression is the major symptom (Example: Tillie Truhart, aspiring writer, gets rejection notices every day and is now so depressed she can't write.

Adjustment Disorder With Disturbed Conduct. Misconduct by violating law or social standards of behavior (Examples: vandalism, passing bad checks, reckless driving, fighting).

Adjustment Disorder With Mixed Disturbance of Emotions and Conduct. Mixed features of anxiety, depression, and misconduct. (Example: John walks out on Mary because of her "constant nagging" then keeps phoning her to reconcile but meanwhile slashes the tires on her car, throws a rock through her window and steals her mail).

Adjustment Disorder With Mixed Emotional Features. Anxiety and depression without misconduct (Example: You quit your job because you "can't take it anymore," then sit home crying because you miss it).

Adjustment Disorder With Physical Complaints. Your body reacts to stress with aches and pains not confirmed by medical examination.

Adjustment Disorder With Withdrawal. Psychological escape into social isolation, running away (Example: Philistine Flugelhorn, aspiring writer, gets rejection notices every day, remains home in her room and refuses all social contacts).

Adjustment Disorder With Work (or Academic) Inhibition. Your previously good work or school performance drops, usually with some accompanying anxiety and depression (Example: Since his wife left him, Hezekiah Huff's production of widgets is down a third).

SEXUAL DISORDERS. There are two types: **paraphilias,** sexual behavior that violates the law or social norms (kinky!), and **sexual**

dysfunction, problems having sex. Both persist for six months or more and they are disturbing to the person with the problem.

Paraphilias

Exhibitionism. An intense urge with erotic fantasies to expose genitalia to an unsuspecting stranger and has done so.

Fetishism. An intense urge with erotic fantasies to obtain (usually steal) intimate garments (bras, panties) and sexually use them, and does so.

Frotteurism. Intense urge with erotic fantasies to touch or rub against an unconsenting person, and does so.

Pedophilia. A person age 16 or older and five years older than the child pursued, with an intense urge with erotic fantasies to have sexual contact with a child usually under 13 years old, and does so.

Sexual Masochism. Intense urge with erotic fantasies to become sexually excited by being beaten, bound, and humiliated and suffer in these ways, and does it.

Sexual Sadism. Intense urge with erotic fantasies to become sexually excited by inflicting pain and humiliation (physical and psychological pain) on a person who is attractive to the sadist, and does so.

Transvestic Fetishist is a heterosexual male with an intense urge and erotic fantasies to dress like a woman and does so.

Voyeurism. A voyeur is a "peeping Tom" with an intense urge to and erotic fantasies of secretly watching a person who is undressing, naked, or having sex, and does so.

Paraphilias Not Otherwise Specified (NOS)
   Telephone scatologia (obscene phone caller)
   Necrophilia (sexual fixation on to corpses)
   Partialism (sexual fixation on a body part, legs, breasts, buttocks, neck, feet, etc.)
   Zoophilia (animals!)
   Coprophilia (defecation)
   Klismaphilia (enemas)
   Urophilia (urination)

Sexual Dysfunctions

Sexual Desire Disorders. Two types: Low sex drive, few erotic fantasies, little desire (**hypoactive sexual desire disorder**); or an extreme aversion to and avoiding all or almost all sexual contact (**sexual aversion disorder**).

Sexual Arousal Disorders: Failure to experience sexual excitement or pleasure having sex. In addition, the woman's vagina does not lubricate (**female sexual arousal disorder**) and men who cannot have or keep an erection (**male sexual arousal disorder**).

Orgasm Disorders. Failure to achieve orgasm even after normal sexual excitement during sexual contact. For women, it's **inhibited female orgasm** and for men **inhibited male orgasm.**

Premature Ejaculation is male orgasm with little or no stimulation or sexual contact, occurring before, just at, or shortly after penetration.

Sexual Pain Disorders. Men or women with genital pain before, during, or after sexual contact; not caused solely by a dry vagina (**dyspareunia**). Women who have an involuntary spasm of muscle in the outer third of the vagina that interferes with having sex (**vaginismus**).

FACTITIOUS DISORDER is intentionally faking symptoms with no other motive than to be sick or to be a patient: if physical symptoms are faked it's **factitious disorder with physical symptoms** and if psychiatric symptoms are faked it's **factitious disorder with psychological symptoms.**

SLEEP DISORDERS occur three or more times per week, for a month or more, and are of three types: **dyssomnia,** difficulty falling asleep; **hypersomnia,** excessive sleepiness; **parasomnia,** disturbed sleep.

Insomnia Disorder Related to Another Mental Disorder (Nonorganic), such as difficulty getting to sleep because of depression or an anxiety disorder; **insomnia disorder related to known organic factor** such as amphetamine dependence or sleep apnea; **primary insomnia,** when not due to organic or functional factors.

Hypersomnia Related to Another Mental Disorder (Nonorganic) such as depression; **hypersomnia related to known organic factor** such as alcohol dependence; **primary hypersomnia** when not due to any organic or functional factor.

Sleep-Wake Schedule Disorder is a disturbance of the "body clock" or circadian rhythm, like jet lag but continuing. If you fall asleep or wake up at inconvenient or unconventional times, it's the **advanced or delayed type;** if you work shifts that rotate and thus disturb your sleep-wake cycle it's the **frequently changing type;** if you don't live a structured, predictable day-night routine and sleeping and waking are haphazard, it's the **disorganized type.**

Parasomnias: Dream Anxiety Disorder is being repeatedly awakened by frightening dreams (nightmares), usually life threatening or humiliating which are remembered and are upsetting upon awakening. **Sleep terror disorder** is recurring, sudden awakening, usually with a scream, intense anxiety, confused, and in physical distress often pounding the pillow or tearing at the bedclothes, and with no memory of the dream's content. **Sleepwalking disorder** is getting up and walking while still asleep, with eyes open trance-like in a blank stare, not easily awakened, but if so, unable to recall any dreams or reason for the event.

There are related sleep disorders not listed in the DSM such as **narcolepsy,** when there are unpredictable "sleep attacks" of 20–40 minutes during which muscles go limp and there are vivid hallucinations for the first few moments; **sleep apnea** where breathing stops completely for about ten seconds, more than thirty times during sleep, with loud snoring and gasping, choking or striking out at the end of each stoppage; **nocturnal myoclonus** is having shock-like muscle jerks during sleep which cause awakening or restless sleep; **restless legs** is a strong urge to move the legs, to get up and walk.

Impulse Control Disorders Not Elsewhere Classified

Intermittent Explosive Disorder, violent, assaultive, or destructive acting out, grossly out of proportion to any cause, and with no impulsive, aggressive behaviors between "explosions."

Kleptomania, recurrent urge to steal what isn't needed, what you could easily buy, and not an angry or vengeful reaction. Tension rises before the theft, is relieved with the theft.

Pathological gambling is excessive gambling with four or more of these: preoccupied with it and getting money to do it; bets more than intended; needs to bet more money more often; edgy if not gambling; if loses, returns promptly to try to win it back; has tried to stop but can't; gambles despite other obligations; continues despite rising debt, home, job, or legal problems related to loss of money.

Pyromania, deliberate fire-setting more than once; fascinated with fire, reads about it, collects material on it; tension and arousal before, satisfaction while watching, relief afterwards; not done for money, as political protest, or part of delusion.

Trichotillomania is the recurring impulse to pull out your hair, with tension before and relief after doing so and when there's no skin irritation to cause it.

PSYCHOACTIVE SUBSTANCE USE DISORDERS. These are listed by the types of substances used and further identified as **dependency** or **abuse**. **Dependency** requires three or more of these: takes more and for a longer time than intended; tried to stop but can't; spends time using it and getting money to buy more; often intoxicated but may briefly stop taking substance to satisfy work, school or home obligations; missing out on social, home, and leisure activities; continues despite knowing risks; needs more and more to get the same high. **Abuse** is substance use which persists more than a month and abuser knows the psychological, social, occupational, and physical problems it causes; poor judgment, uses it in high-risk situations (driving, operating machinery).

Treatable Nonmental Disorders

The DSM also lists "conditions not attributable to a mental disorder that are the focus of attention or treatment" such as academic problems, borderline intellectual function (between mild mental retardation and dull normal or low average intelligence), child, adolescent or adult antisocial behavior, parent-child, occupational, family, marital, phase of life or other interpersonal problems, and "uncomplicated bereavement" (normal grieving).

DSM Overview—and Minisermon!

Most DSM disorders can be further described by **onset** (early or late), **duration** (acute, meaning sudden; chronic, meaning longterm), and **severity** or intensity (mild, moderate, severe). The DSM uses a menu or checklist system and NOS (not otherwise specified) to identify conditions most like others but not a perfect fit. Having all listed symptoms at all times is not needed to qualify for a particular diagnosis. In fact, the vast majority of the mentally ill look and behave like you and me. A joke often told in mental hospitals is that "you can't tell the staff from the patients." Years ago that was funny because staff seemed "crazier" than patients. Today, due to more effective medications and therapy patients do not seem "crazy" at all and so look and behave like the staff. Thankfully, this isn't such a joking matter any more.

You really shouldn't use words like "crazy, psycho, whacko, looney, maniac, nut." They're not scientific terms, and since reading this book you're going to be more scientific, right? Using those slang words is really name-calling, demeaning, and dehumanizing. Better words: angry, frightened, upset, depressed, confused, anxious—DSM language, **scientific** language. Review the symptoms described in this chapter and you'll see yourself at one time or another in your life. As the saying goes, "but for the grace of God go I." Finally, don't try to be a Freud and put labels on your friends, family, and coworkers. That's just another form of name-calling, and it's a good way to lose friends and along with it some of your own integrity. You ain't Freud!

WHAT HAVE YOU LEARNED?

This chapter described "them"—the personalities and behaviors of the people you will be observing and questioning. "Normal" personalities were described in terms of three major theories (**psychoanalytic, behaviorist, humanistic**), Horney's **four selves,** and **defense mechanisms** used to avoid reality. Abnormal behavior was described by **neurotic needs** and adult **mental disorders** from the latest diagnostic manual (DSM). Mental disorders are **organic** (physical) or **functional** (psychological). Functional disorders were sorted into three categories: **psychosis, personality disorders,** and **reactive disorders.**

You should have learned a great deal about **yourself** in this chapter. "Normal" people have one or more disturbed thoughts and feelings which are the same as those of the mentally ill. "Normal" and abnormal are a matter of degree (severity), not kind. This chapter should enable you to better understand the thoughts, feelings, and behaviors of "them" —those you will interview or interrogate. The longer you question people, the more you will see everything described in this chapter.

If this chapter achieved its goal, you now see more clearly and more deeply into human nature, in yourself and in others you observe every day. This will make you more comfortable (and **comforting**) to others as you see into and through them. Hopefully, you are more relaxed with yourself because you understand yourself better and can accept yourself more. If, on the other hand, anything in the chapter raised questions or concerns about yourself, things you never saw before and which may be upsetting to you, share them with a someone you trust and can confide in. There are also community mental health centers, helplines, and private practitioners ethically bound to maintain confidentiality and protect your privacy. And, if you're now fascinated with human nature, eager to learn more about the mind and behavior, here are some additional readings and references:

American Psychiatric Association. *Diagnostic and Statistical Manual of Mental Disorders.* Latest edition. Washington, DC: American Psychiatric Press, Inc.
(*This is the standard reference for the identification and classification of mental disorders and a valuable resource to have close at hand. There is a pocket-sized version entitled Desk Reference to the Diagnostic Criteria from DSM but it is best to get the full-sized latest edition of the DSM. Source: American Psychiatric Press, Inc., 1400 K Street NW, Washington DC 20005*).
Drapela, V. J. (1987). *A Review of Personality Theories.* Springfield, IL: Charles C Thomas.
(*This 166-page book is a concise overview of the major personality theories. Source: Charles C Thomas Publisher, 2600 South First Street, Springfield, IL 62794-9265*).
Dubovsky, S. L. (1988). *Concise Guide to Clinical Psychiatry.* Washington DC: American Psychiatric Press, Inc.
(*An excellent companion volume to the DSM because it further describes mental disorders, their treatment and the latest "state of the art" of psychiatric theory and practice. Source: American Psychiatric Press, Inc. Complete address is listed above*).
Vaillant, G. E. (1986). *Empirical Studies of Ego Mechanisms of Defense.* Washington DC: American Psychiatric Press, Inc.
(*More than you ever wanted to know about defense mechanisms but important because it contains the latest research on them and indepth definitions from leading researchers so that you can thoroughly understand them. Source: American Psychiatric Press, Inc. Complete address listed above*).

Chapter 3

INTERACTION

> He that has eyes to see and ears to hear
> may convince himself that no mortal
> can keep a secret. If his lips are silent
> he chatters with his fingertips and
> betrayal oozes out of him at every pore.
> Sigmund Freud (1905)

Interaction, interpersonal communications, involves nonverbal and verbal behaviors. Nonverbal behavior, known also as body talk, body language, or kinesics, is what people do with their bodies while conversing. Verbal behavior includes not only what is said, word choice and use, but also loudness, softness, emphasis, speed of delivery, and the use of silences and pauses. Effective, **scientific** interview and interrogation are not as much **what** you say as **how** you say it.

Nonverbal Behavior

There is no thought or feeling you can have without communicating it in some way through your body, by posture, gestures, and mannerisms, by how you look at a person, where you look, facial expression, even where and how close you are to others. Underlying thoughts and feelings can be detected by close observation and interpreted according to when and how often they occur (**frequency**), and how forceful they are (**intensity, range of motion**). There are individual differences, and exceptions, and some can be due to culture and nationality. Many Italians **do** "talk with their hands," but some do not. Japanese tend to use few hand gestures while speaking. Most Europeans eat with the knife kept in the right hand, using the fork in their left. They find it humorous that Americans keep switching, cutting with the knife in the right hand then changing to the fork. This mannerism has been used in spy movies to detect American undercover agents. It **is** an easily observable distinctive nonverbal behavior. Some families are more demonstrative, showing affection with hugs and kisses, others seldom if ever do so.

Incredible as it may seem, one expert claims you are capable of 250,000 different facial expressions—without saying a word (Birdwhistell, 1970). In 1873, Charles Darwin commented that gestures are "an elaborate and secret code that is written nowhere, known by none, and understood by all." What is **your** nonverbal communications style? It can be **imitative** if you learned it from birth through family life to the present, **instinctive** if natural and spontaneous and you 'go with the flow" of feelings, or **selective** if you choose or select when to use it and when not to. For interviewing and interrogating this is the recommended style since it requires that you screen your behavior, are aware of its potential effect, and more judiciously use it as a technique.

EXERCISE 9

How "physical" are you with your nonverbal behavior? Do you "talk with your hands" or do you seldom use body movement when you talk with others? Does your family use more or fewer body movements when communicating with others? How does your nonverbal behavior compare with your coworkers or friends? How much is cultural? How much is due to sex role behavior (if you're a woman and they are men, and vice versa)? Are you overly physical? Inhibited? If so, why? Can/should you do more or less nonverbal behavior? This is an important question and it will take all the content of this chapter to help you answer it.

Place, Time, Space

Where and when something happens can be as important as **what** happens there. **Place behavior** or **situation-specific behavior** is what happens and is expected in certain narrowly focussed situations. As the old saying goes, "there's a time and place for everything." Generally, people at funerals are solemn, at weddings lighthearted, while shopping preoccupied. Women bank tellers don't usually have low-cut dresses showing cleavage, and bank managers don't wear colorful sport shirts. A male bank teller was referred to me once by his employer for counseling because he wore red socks! In an elevator, you're supposed to be serious, face forward, and look at the floor indicator atop the doorway and not at others. While standing close in a waiting line, or seated in a restaurant close to others, it's impolite to listen to what strangers discuss. The same is true in doctor and dentist waiting rooms. When you **do** speak in any of these situations, only a brief exchange on safe subjects is expected.

EXERCISE 10

Try talking to someone in any of the situations described above. It is an ideal opportunity to communicate with a stranger on safe, neutral ground, in a time-limited brief encounter. Observe their nonverbal behaviors: eye contact, gestures and mannerisms, body placement, and movement. This will help you to compare nonverbal behaviors of people under the stress of interview or interrogation and to know the difference, what is a significant behavioral cue or clue and what is just a normal variation.

Time and **timing** are very important factors in interview and interrogation. Examples of how time influences behavior are jet lag, changing shifts, hangovers, and the rush to meet deadlines. There is a flow to conversation and everyone speaks and thinks at an individual, natural speed. As Zen Buddhists say, "don't push the river." There can be regional or cultural differences such as city vs rural or deep South and northern big city, but this is an oversimplification—there are many exceptions. Sales persons are stereotyped as "fast talkers" and many are, but not all. Notice that when they are fast talkers they are also called "high pressure." To effectively question anyone you must pace yourself to their speed of thought and speech, then move in to accelerate or slow them. Speed up and you apply stress, like the fast-talking salesperson. Slow down and you invite a deeper, shared probe, and you also give bright psychopaths more time to outwit you. It is important to know how to use **time** and **timing** to your advantage.

The river of the mind, yours and mine, flows at a certain speed. To understand others and for most interview settings, don't push the river. To interrogate, always do so. This can be done with speech, by comment or question. In some cases it is more effective to do it with silence, doing nothing, just freezing and sitting with no other nonverbal behaviors. Actors and actresses call this "artistic repose." It has been described as "the gentle art of doing nothing." Silence is a very powerful technique ("the crash of silence") and most interviewers and interrogators do not use it enough. Many confessions have resulted from an uncomfortable, electric silence.

EXERCISE 11

Experiment with silences, with coworkers, friends, and family, in everyday conversation. When you use silence, keep eye contact but do not use any other nonverbal behaviors. Shift into mental neutral, freeze, do nothing else. See how long it takes them to "catch on" then ask them what effect the silence had on them. Did they take your silence to mean you disagreed with them? Misunderstood them? How uncomfortable were they with it?

Space is more than mood and attitude. It is like an aura or magnetic field around you, an electrical charge in the air, radiating from your thoughts, feelings, and personality. You can assess someone's space by how they arrange the "stuff" of their life such as home and office furnishings. Some people arrange their work space like a spider web with themselves in the center. Others use wide desks with chairs for others across the front to keep everyone at a distance. The more "people-centered" put desks against the wall and sit beside you. Generally, desk "clutter," the way papers are spread across a desk top, and the way files are maintained, is a measure of how organized that person is mentally. The same is true of living room furniture. Wall colors, art, and bric-a-brac tell you much about what is important to that individual.

Psychological distance is a factor of mental space. There is a distance, physical and mental, between you and everyone else and it varies with the situation, time available, and mood of "space." In the old movies, police stood and suspects sat, under a bright light, in a plain room with little furniture. We have learned that **less psychological distance** is far more effective than the old "third degree." Sitting side-by-side or knee-to-knee, interrogator leaning forward and with physical touching is more "open" psychologically, sharing as equals, conducive to "soul searching" and "unburdening the soul"—confession. Observe people seated at meetings or religious services, when several sit on a long sofa, and note the distance between them. Generally, they do not touch and observe a certain "safe" distance. Observe any two people talking together and note the distance between their faces. This, too, is a certain comfortable distance.

EXERCISE 12

In a safe, neutral setting, while talking with a coworker, friend, or family member, move in just a little bit closer, continuing the conversation as you normally would, with a slightly lower voice. If this is not detected by the other person, continue very slowly to move in closer. If they do not bring this to your attention, stop the conversation and explain what you did and why (don't confuse 'em). Discuss what effect this closer distance had on the conversation.

EXERCISE 13

With another person, select a safe topic (weather, current event, favorite vacation place, car, or food). With a stopwatch, talk together for five minutes without using personal pronouns (I, you, he, she, we, us, they, them). Point out each time either violates this rule but don't keep score. During the five minutes most people get increasingly irritated and frustrated at a conversation that becomes colder, less personal. That feeling is psychological distance.

Costumes, Ornaments, Roles, Props

Everybody wears a costume! Some, like military, police, airline pilots and stewardesses, food servers, white-collared clergy, or hotel staff, are easily recognized. Some add a costume to their street clothes, like doctors with short white coats. Men wearing business suits, shirts, and ties are in uniform. Whatever you wear on the job that you don't normally wear at home is very likely to be your costume. The psychological function is to project a particular image. Airline pilot uniforms send a "take charge nothing can go wrong" message. White-coated doctors and nurses project a "scrubbed, squeaky clean, disease-free" setting. Men and women lawyers with business suits and leather briefcases radiate a "don't screw with me! Can't you *see* I *look like* I know what I'm doing" message. Uniformed police send the message: "I got a gun and a badge, so don't do anything wrong." As we know, the number of visible uniformed police officers and well-marked police cars lessen the incidence of crime. Criminals have used costumes to more easily commit crimes, such as hotel thieves dressed as clergy, police, or military officers, workmen, or business men with attache cases.

You are wearing a costume right now! If at work, take a good look at yourself. What message are you sending by what you wear? If at home, what you're wearing tells the keen observer your "mental space" or how you want it to be (why did you dress like that?). Even if you're in bed you're in a sleeping costume (if nude *that's* your sleeping costume, your "birthday suit"). We are judged by what we wear. Cab drivers and truck drivers dress casually, doctors, lawyers, and business executives don't. If a lawyer showed up in court in a jogging outfit or a surgeon made hospital rounds in a swimsuit, there would at least be stares. On the other hand, people expect less formal, even garish clothing on famous artists, writers, or composers.

Even underwear is a costume. Men wear boxer or jockey shorts, white or colored. Women wear bras, panties, or pantyhose. Color and style can be highly individualized to the personality of the wearer. Extremes can tell much about the personality—if a man wears women's clothing, chances are he's a transvestite. Hair style is part of costuming. Some hospitals require that nurses' hair be short enough so as not to touch the collar. Some armed forces have a similar regulation for both men and women. Women with very short hair can project as "mannish" and men with long hair can be seen as "effeminate." Women are expected to wear face makeup but men are not. A business suit on the beach or a swimsuit in church would draw attention. There are very real and relatively rigid rules for clothing and appearance. Within these limits, we try to reflect our own unique personality by clothing, from underwear to outerwear, and with jewelry and makeup. Effective interviewers and interrogators observe these individual differences to better understand the unique personality of the wearer.

Ornaments are signs of identification or insignia worn with the costumes such as rings, pins, bracelets, earrings, and other similar objects. Like costumes, ornaments project messages to others of how the wearer wants to be perceived. Engagement and wedding rings tell the world: "I'm taken, spoken for." School, fraternal, and military rings and pins say "look where I've been" or "see who I am." Massive rings and jewelry "talk" louder. Expensive jewelry can be subtle put-downs of others ("See how rich I am") or special ("See how much somebody loves me"). The number of diamonds in a man's ring denotes rank within the organization in a criminal syndicate. Jewelry can facilitate conversation, projecting the message: "I'm shy. Please ask me about this jewelry." Exotic, unusual jewelry says: "I'm an interesting person, ask me." Men wear less jewelry than women, so they **compensate** with distinctive ties, shirts, belt buckles or shoes. Tattoos are permanent body ornamentation, usually individualized by symbol or name.

Props are types of ornaments which further differentiates you from others, such as police or company cars, computers, briefcases and attache cases, guns and badges, tools, equipment, beeper pagers, hand-held radios, even distinctive pens—or the number of them displayed in the pocket. Props project messages describing your importance or specialized knowledge and skill: "Look at what I got! Only I know how to use it." Criminals have used props to attract victims, such as the serial killer who wore a fake cast on his arm in a shopping mall, asking for help to his car, thieves and rapists wearing coveralls and carrying tools, sometimes even official looking ID, or the hotel thief dressed as a priest carrying a Bible or with sunglasses and white cane faking being blind. Many professional contract killers are experts at using deceptive costumes and props to avoid suspicion.

EXERCISE 14

Open your clothes closet and jewelry box and take a good look. What image or personality do your clothes and jewelry project? Look especially at the predominant style, what you wear most frequently. Is it the real you?

Roles or **role behavior** is "acting" a part rather than being the **real you**, submerging your personality in a job or life situation. Married women can find themselves in the role of mother, childcare worker, cook, housekeeper, wife, lover, and also in a full-time occupation. Men can assume several roles in the same job. A manager can be a technical expert, team leader, father confessor, and accountant. The effect of these many roles is to blur the edge of individuality to the point you wonder which role is the real you. The psychiatrist, Carl Jung, described role behavior in terms of the **persona,** a "mask" worn to enact a role. It is automatic, routine, repetitive behavior not at all individualized, like a bank teller counting money, an accountant on the computer, airline pilot at the controls. It's "doing your **thing**" in a specific job, not "doing **your** thing." Jung also taught the **anima-animus** concept, that in every man there are some feminine traits (**anima**), in every woman some masculine traits (**animus**). Examples: The President should have heroic courage in foreign affairs (**animus**) but a caring attitude toward those in need (**anima**). Much of this role behavior is the result of culture and tradition ("It's a man's world"). It is important for you to realize that you are a **person** and not a **persona,** more **real** than **role** regardless of where you are at work or at home.

EXERCISE 15

Analyze your role and role behaviors by listing your job title and the various roles you perform on the job. Add other roles at home and in your leisure time activities. Take a good look at them. Are they consistent or different? Which more closely fit the real you? How could any of them influence your style of questioning in interview and interrogation?

Body Placement, Posture, Movement

Place is where the body is, the location in a room and the chair chosen. **Posture** is how the body stands or sits. **Movement** is the nature and variety of gestures and mannerisms. Given a wide selection of places to stand or sit, people generally choose what is most comfortable for them according to their mood at the moment. This varies in different situations at different times, though most of us have a fixed pattern of where we like to sit. Most people are uncomfortable sitting in the first row in church. Theatre seats sell out in the center first. Most people crowd forward at a special event in which they're interested. Shy people tend to sit where there are fewer seats and lights. Suspicious, fearful, or cynical people usually choose seats where they can watch everyone. The timid and also the paranoid, like to sit at or near the door or aisle, for quick escape. Ambitious, political types or those who feel the need to sell themselves or some cause or product, tend to sit where they can best be the center of attention. You may find it helpful to have more than enough chairs in your interview or interrogation room and let the person to be questioned enter the room first, observing which chair is chosen.

EXERCISE 16

Where is your favorite seat in a theater? Restaurant? Religious service? Friend's home? Your own home? How is furniture placed in your living room? Why? What's your favorite chair? Why?

EXERCISE 17

In your everyday life, begin observing where people sit in: buses, trains and airliners; theaters and restaurants; hotel lobbies; bars and lounges; religious services; park benches; waiting rooms; court, hearings. Observe where and how people walk on the street. Who walks closest to the curb? To building walls?

Posture or **posturing,** how you stand and sit, is another important nonverbal behavior. Little Cuthbert meets Daddy at the front door and says: "Watch out, Mom's mad!" Daddy asks how he knows that. "I know she's mad," Cuthbert confides, "because she **walks** mad!" How you **walk** can project how you feel: a tired shuffle, proud strut, nervous pacing, relaxed stroll. How you **sit** can project feelings: apprehensive, as if your backbone was a steel rod, with quick, short hand gestures; relaxed, slouched with arms and legs spread; attentive and involved, leaning forward, head up, eyes on what's happening; guarded, sitting upright with arms folded, legs crossed against the speaker or questioner. How you **stand** also can signal feelings: nervous or impatient, with toe tapping, fidgeting with pen or paper; relaxed, arms casually at your side, slow, easy gestures; angry, with tense muscles, feet parted, looking authoritative. Your best position for interview and interrogation is to **ground** or **center** yourself, sitting upright but comfortably, your body weight equally distributed over the seat, both feet flat on the floor, your calf and thigh at right angles. This is a stable, balanced position for most effective breathing and helps you to be less prone to nervous posturing and mannerisms.

Movement and **mannerisms** are signals with arms, hands, legs, feet, head, and body of thoughts and feelings, like ships flashing coded messages at sea. Here are the more common signals: Squirming; restless rocking or repetitive movement of foot; fidgeting with hair, clothing, rings, pins, pen, belt, or buckle; twiddling thumbs; tapping or drumming fingers; tightly clasped hands or clenched fists; folded arms; emphatic gestures like pointing finger or upraised or waved hand; picking at body, fingers, or nailbiting; fine hand tremors; scratching; touching face or mouth; sighing or yawning; irregular breathing; eyelid flutter; teary eyes; blank stare; twitching (mouth); squinting or furrowed brow; giggling, nervous laughter, or silly behavior; constant chatter or nervously scanning the room; slowing speech; silences; sniffling; shrugging; shifting in the chair; picking teeth; swallowing; foot tapping; clearing the throat or nervous coughing; quick, jerky head movements; mouth or tongue movement; flared nostrils; spitting; chain smoking or putting out half smoked or just lit cigarettes; gum chewing or compulsive nibbling eating. These may be **baseline behaviors,** everyday mannerisms, not signalling anxiety because of your questioning and not important to the interview or interrogation process. But if they occur *only* when certain questions are asked or specific subjects discussed, they should *always* alert you to probe further.

Gestures are a kind of body movement, further classified into three types: **manipulators, emblems,** and **illustrators.** A **manipulator** is any kind of **nervous fidgeting** (manipulative), such as picking lint off clothes, teasing hair, pulling ears, rubbing, squeezing, or grooming. Hands or fingers are most often involved. Manipulators have no meaning other than to signal the nervousness that causes them. Many are learned behaviors from parents or others. An **emblem** is a gesture that **gives a message without words,** such as a shrug of the shoulders meaning "I don't know," up-and-down head nodding for "No," side-to-side for "yes," thumb up of V for victory with index and middle finger separated for "OK," or the infamous "bird" or "screw you" of an upraised middle finger. An **illustrator** is a gesture that dramatizes or increases the impact of what is said, such as pointing an index finger, snapping the fingers, a wave of the hand, or raised eyebrows.

Key factors in evaluating body movement are when they occur (at what point in questioning), how often (similar question or subject), their intensity or force, their speed, and range or sweep of motion. When you are nervous, your muscles tense up. The higher the anxiety, the tighter the muscles. That's why relaxation therapy, meditation, and hypnosis help relieve stress and excessive fears (like phobias). "Uptight" people have tight muscles, and because of this, their gestures are likely to be quick and jerky. If your questioning increases their anxiety level, it is likely you will see some resulting body movement.

EXERCISE 18

How does your body react to stress? What is your body's weak link? Under stress, are you aware of any posturing or mannerisms you have? Try centering or grounding yourself as described above to reduce nervous posturing and mannerisms. You will want to be in a neutral, stable position when questioning others.

Head, Face, Masks

You **see** someone **before** you speak with them. First impressions can be deceiving, misleading. As you learned in earlier chapters, it is important to be **scientific**, to see what's there and not what you want or expect to see, to allow the **real self** to be seen.

Heads are important behavioral clues by their movement. Approval or disapproval by nodding the head vertically or horizontally is international and cross-cultural. Surprise or understanding what is said is often shown by nodding the head backwards as if to say: "Yes, I see." A slow nod may mean uncertainty or mild disagreement or just a sign that you are listening attentively to what is said to you. A tilted head, like a dog hearing a strange noise, means the listener is fascinated or a bit puzzled, and can also be a seductive come-on.

Faces may well be the most expressive parts of the body. We speak of "facing up to the truth, losing or saving face, having a sad or long face, poker face, sourpuss, and face-to-face confrontations." Untruthful persons are "bare faced liars." Faces can be easily read, such as someone blushing from embarrassment or self-consciousness, or "deadpan," without expression, like the proverbial poker player. Faces are further distinguished by being bordered with hair of a specific color, length, texture, and arranged in an individual style. Skin is of a distinctive color and complexion (blacks are not **black** and whites are not **white**). Faces become **masks** when the **real self** does not emerge through it such as under severe stress ("a mask of fear"), bring very bored, when heavily into role behavior, manipulating others, or trying to be "all things to all people," and being nobody. A smiling face radiates positive feeling through the curved mouth, bright eyes, raised eyebrows, and arching head movement.

Eyes are expressive, sensitive to and broadcasting inner feelings. Buddha described them as "windows of the soul." On an operating table, the surgeon's eyes alone can be reassuring even though you can't see the whole face. Eyes can be intense or distracted, happy or sad, light or heavy, clear or glazed. We speak of "bedroom eyes, a come hither look, icy stare, evil eye, fish eye, far-away look," and "if looks could kill," and "as if you've swallowed the canary." Some women say "he was undressing me with his eyes." When people are nervous, they tend to blink their eyes, squint, stare, glance more quickly up, down, or around the room, or show eyelid flutter or tears. **Eye contact** is the number and length of time glances are exchanged and is a sensitive marker of underlying feelings. The "light" or "fire" in the eyes reflect one's interest and understanding of what's happening, boredom with it, or a wink to "make a pass" or "sexual overture" without saying anything verbally. The eyes of hardened criminals tend to be cold, distant, calculating, uncaring; those of crime victims like those of frightened animals or hurt children.

More than fifty years of research confirm that it is possible to recognize "pleasant" from "unpleasant" facial expressions with a high degree of accuracy (Ekman, Friesen & Ellsworth, 1972). Research also shows that facial expressions can be faked, like lie detectors, truth serum, and hypnosis. But these scientific studies show that under stress it is far more difficult to conceal underlying emotions. The most accurate interpretations are based on careful observation of both audio (verbal) and visual (nonverbal) behaviors, far better than either audio or visual alone. By close observation of **all** behavior, careful selection of questions and when and how to ask them, reflected against a knowledge of the person questioned and of human nature, you will greatly increase the effectiveness of your interviewing and interrogation.

Mouths are important communicators even without speech. The *Mona Lisa* may be the most famous mouth in history and continues to pose a mystery as to what she was thinking or feeling the time the portrait was painted. Smiles light up the face and involve the eyes, eyebrows, and head. A broad smile with lips parted and teeth showing usually suggests a person who is less guarded, more open. A partial smile with closed lips suggests shyness and uncertainty. There is a distinctive smile of embarrassment and one of satisfaction, "like the cat who just swallowed the mouse." Forced smiles, "frozen" or "tightlipped" smiles, usually betray high anxiety, hostility, or a rigid, unyielding attitude. Some crime victims have commented on the "sick smile" of the criminal, a kind of "devilish grin." The mouth can be sensuous, and kissing is an example of how the mouth expresses love and caring. Even from a distance, pursed lips in a pucker can "throw a kiss."

EXERCISE 19

Watching TV as you normally do, observe how actors and actresses use facial expressions and head movement to portray various emotions. Without being conspicuous, observe various facial expressions of people at work, shopping, and on the street. Try to read their feelings only by facial expression before they speak. TV and your everyday observations can help you increase your awareness and understanding of nonverbal behavior.

Touch

Touch or **tactile communication** is another means of nonverbal behavior. As a newborn baby it is the first sensory message you receive. Hopefully, you were lovingly, gently placed in a dry, warm, comfortable little bed and rocked and patted. Touch is nonverbal and universal, used by all the peoples of the world throughout history. Of all the senses, touch is the least used in everyday adult communication. Even though we see how much children enjoy being held, rocked, hugged, and reassured by a gentle pat, as grownups we stiffen with embarrassment if someone suddenly invades our space with an unexpected or unwanted touch. Many of us even force a hug or kiss to family members to whom we do not feel especially close. Some couples touch only sexually and this in time can become artificial and mechanical.

Not receiving enough physical touching as a baby and young child can cause psychological and emotional problems. Called **stroke hunger, touch hunger, emotional skin hunger,** or **tactile deprivation,** it can lead to slowed emotional development, low self-concept and self-consciousness; less body weight, low stress threshold and resulting higher anxiety level, less resistance to disease, bedwetting, nailbiting, and exaggerated fears.

Why are we afraid to touch? Some of us are raised in families who avoid touching. There can be many other reasons: low self-concept (feel you don't deserve to be loved); fear of physical contact (if abused in early, formative years); poor body image (ashamed of your body). When we are touched, it is usually not as a show of affection, and always in "safe" nonerotic places, such as being helped in or out of crowded or precarious places, prevented from stepping off the curb into traffic, by barbers and beauticians, doctors or nurses. "Safe" touching can be on the hand, arm, shoulder, or elbow and is done lightly, casually, and quickly. Linger for a few seconds and the touch can be misinterpreted. A firm touch is reassuring, like holding one's hand. Many experienced police, military, and intelligence interrogators make physical contact with those they question. They sit close to them, and from time to time place a reassuring hand on their knee or shoulder. Many confessions have been facilitated with the interrogator's arm around the suspect's shoulder.

EXERCISE 20

Observe small children. They can teach you a great deal about natural, caring, nonsexual touching. Watch them, how they touch without thinking about it, hug, sit close, share physical warmth and mutual support.

EXERCISE 21

Think back, when was the last time you had physical contact with someone? Who, where, why? A person or a pet? If both, how is the touch different for each? Why? If a person, was it a child or an adult? How does the touching differ? Do you really know the difference between sexual and nonsexual touch? Has your touching ever been misinterpreted?

Autonomic Signs

Everyone has an autonomic or **automatic** nervous system. It is involuntary, beyond conscious control, and knowing it gives you valuable information about the person's anxiety state during questioning. It has two branches. During waking hours **sympathetic nervous system** predominates and when asleep the **parasympathetic nervous system** is in control. It is the sympathetic branch that stimulates us to fight, fright, or flight. The polygraph machine measures three of its body signs: breathing, heart rate, and skin conductivity. You can observe many more and you should develop your awareness of them and be alert for them: sweating; erect body hair ("hair bristles"); "gooseflesh"; cold clammy hands; rapid or irregular breathing; bobbing Adam's apple; startle reflex (jumpy, jerky); twitches and tremors; churning or "butterflies" stomach; diarrhea; nausea.

EXERCISE 22

What's your body's "weak link" under stress? Where do you feel it when you're in a crisis situation? Some feel it in the stomach, tight or churning. Others get cold, clammy hands, or a pounding heart or headache. You should know your body's weak spot because in a stressful interview or interrogation your body can be an "early warning system" to alert you to your rising anxiety. It is then you should **center** or **ground**

yourself or take a break to "plateau out" the anxiety. You can't do your best if you don't feel well. Take care of yourself!

Nonverbal Shorthand

You can write when and how nonverbal behaviors occur as you take notes of what is said in your interview or interrogation. The following is a suggested system of shorthand which abbreviates each body part. Use parentheses or encircle this nonverbal shorthand to separate it from your notes of the person's answers to questions. In this way it can easily be seen when you review your notes, clues to key responses. Use small arrows to show direction of movement of the body part, like a nod of the head up and down, and larger arrows for longer range of motion, like a sweeping gesture of a hand or an arm swinging. The letter V with an arrow up or down signifies a raised or lowered voice. Use L or R to indicate LEFT or RIGHT. A simple drawn teardrop marks when a person started weeping. Inserting this shorthand in your notes will enable you to see when and how nonverbal behavior occurred in connection with specific questions or references to events or subjects. Using shorthand saves time and does not interfere with your concentration or note-taking as in writing longhand. With a little practice, you'll be able to observe nonverbal behavior, note it, and take down what is said. This classification system is also a good review of which body parts are most used in nonverbal behavior:

H or He = head	Ar or Arm = arm
Hr = hair	Ha = hand
Fa = face	Fi = finger
Mo = mouth	Ri = ring
No = nose	Cl = clothing
Li = lip	El = elbow
To = tongue	Kn = knee
Ey = eye	Th = thigh
Eyb = eyebrow	Fo or FT = foot
Ne or Nk = neck	Sh = shoe
Br = breathing rate	Sw = sweating

One of the simplest ways to understand verbal interaction with others is **transactional analysis** or TA, a personality theory and system of analyzing behavior founded in 1957 by Eric Berne, and further developed in his 1964 book *Games People Play* and later by Thomas Harris in his 1967 book *I'm OK—You're OK* and others. Whenever people interact, they also **transact** "mental business," and those transactions can be analyzed. Harris called TA "a blueprint of the mind." What follows is the author's version of the major ideas of this theory.

Verbal Behavior

Transactions. We all play games, verbal games, word games. A **transaction** is an exchange of strokes. Whatever you say or do, verbal or nonverbal, to another person is a **stroke**. An exchange of strokes is a **transaction**. Everyone needs strokes. If you don't get enough of them you can have **stroke hunger.** Strokes are of three types: **warm fuzzies**, positive, caring, and supportive; **cold pricklies**, negative, rejecting, and destructive; **plastic fuzzies**, artificial, phoney, a verbal "con." Examples: "Is that a new suit (or dress)? You look great" (warm fuzzy). "Is that the best you can do? (cold prickly). To a person you despise: "Good to see you" (plastic fuzzy). If you say this last one to someone you like, it would be a warm fuzzy. Each of us likes to be stroked in a special way: "Different strokes for different folks." Some abused children lie to defend parents who beat them. In such cases, it seems that "negative strokes are better than no strokes at all." A **game** is when an exchange of strokes hurts someone physically or mentally.

P–A–C ego States. Strokes come from one of three **ego states** in your personality and are aimed at an ego state in the person with whom you are transacting: **Parent, Adult,** or **Child.** In TA, these words are always capitalized. Though many TA experts deny it, the ego states are similar to Freud's **superego, ego,** and **id.** Let's look closely at each:

Parent or P is the force within you that plays like an audiotape telling you what you should, ought, or must do. By the time you are five years old your Parent has taped 25,000 hours of what's right or wrong from your real life parents and significant others in your life. That's a lot. The tape plays automatically whenever you're in a situation where you must decide what to do. The Parent is of two types, positive (+P) and negative (−P) and is shown as a capital letter P in a circle, with a + and a − sign on either side of the P.

The **positive Parent** or +**Parent** is like a loving real-life parent, and God is usually pictured as this kind of parental figure. It is caring, nurturing, understanding, accepting, and is the source of your own internal standard of conduct, your morals, ethics, and values. NONVERBAL CLUES: an approving nod, wink, pat, hug, touch, kiss, smile, or look; Christmas trees, birthday parties, gifts, Thanksgiving turkey. VERBAL CLUES: "Great! You did well. Good. You're OK. That's nice. Uh-huh. Yes." Warm fuzzies!

The **negative Parent** or −**Parent** is the flip side, blaming, cold, critical, nitpicking, suspicious, rigid, condescending, overprotective, preachy. If +P is God, −P is not the Devil—that's down in part of the Child. It's more like a vengeful God, perhaps the god of war and misery. NONVERBAL CLUES: horrified look, icy stare ("gallows transaction"); long sigh; disapproving nod; pursed, tight lips; furrowed brow; foot tapping hands on hip; pointing finger; slapping or hitting. VERBAL CLUES: "Not again! I told you so! I'm only trying to help you. Some day you'll thank me. No dessert 'til you clean your plate. Why can't you do it right? Be sure you wear clean underwear—you could be in an accident and they'll know at the hospital what kind of home you come from."

The **Adult** or **A** is shown as the letter A encircled and placed beneath and touching the Parent. Your Adult begins when you first realize the **you** from the **not you,** when you become a person. For most of us, that's about ten months of age. You grab and shake a rattle and know the rattle isn't you but your hand *is* you. The Adult is "caught in the middle" between Parent and Child. If you're mature, your Adult is a good manager, mediator, negotiator, interpreter, and friend. Your Adult takes risks, makes decisions, and wrestles with problems despite the Parent's nagging and the Child's wish to have fun. It's the part of you that learns from experience, and so it's also an efficient data processing computer. NONVERBAL CLUES: Thoughtful, reflective, calm, alert and aware, flexible, listens to self and others, open to criticism, learns by doing, maintains physical and mental health. VERBAL CLUES: "Do you mean . . . could it be . . . I wonder if . . . on the other hand . . . but it seems to me that . . . I disagree, let me explain . . . " in a calm voice, centered, sincere, well grounded. Rudyard Kipling summed up the Adult well: "I have six honest serving men; they serve me good and true; their names are What and Why and When and How and Where and Who." The Adult within you asks good questions, open and unbiased, to learn and grow and find the truth. Your Parent applies the truth. Your Child appeals the decision!

The **Child** is where your feelings are and there are two sides to it: the

+Child or **OK Kid** and the **−Child** or **Not OK Kid.** Most TA experts refer to the OK Kid as the **natural Child** and the Not OK Kid as the **adapted Child.** The Child is shown as the letter C in a circle placed beneath and touching the Adult, and with a + and − sign on either side of the C. It is "put down" by the Parent's rules and the Adult's management and control. The Ok Kid is that beautiful child within you. It is natural, genuine, open, curious, creative, imaginative, fun loving, energetic, sharing, sensual, and indulgent. It can have loud fun or spend hours in an absorbing hobby. TA theory has done more to explain the source and nature of creativity and also uninhibited sex—both are in the OK Kid. NONVERBAL CLUES: boundless energy, chatter, singing and shouting, eating sweets forever unless stopped, giggles and laughter, playful teasing, sharing, hugging, touching, kissing. VERBAL CLUES: "Wow! Gee" Can I, can I? Let's. I wanna. Wudja?"

Your Child is indulgent and "never knows when to stop." If you're on a strict diet, it's your OK Kid that stops your eyes on the restaurant menu at the hot fudge sundae. Immediately your Parent tape says: "Don't even think about it!" The Adult chimes in: "Well, we could have a light supper." At that instant there's an automatic "No!" from the Parent and a giggly "Yeah!" from the Child. Who wins? How much you weigh might tell you! Your OK Kid is delightfully irresponsible. It fibs. Lily Tomlin tells the story of a little girl shopping with her mother who buys a box of animal crackers. When they get home, the box has but one cookie in it. "This box was full when we left the store. I remember shaking it, and it felt full. What happened?" Almost always you get a nonverbal shrug and innocent look from very big eyes, and the universal kid defense almost sung and very slow: "I dunno." But this little girl's OK Kid, with a little bit of reasoning from her small Adult, and looking and sounding very profound said: "Well, see, this last cookie is an elephant and it probly et up all the others." That's how you get to eat the hot fudge sundae!

Your Child is indulgent. Its values are in its tummy, its "eyes are bigger than its stomach." Little Tillie raids the cookie jar when Mommy's away, eats 'em all, gets sick and then punished. If your OK Kid talked with Tillie's, the conversation would go like this:

YOU: So what happened to you, Tillie?

TILLIE (brushing away crocodile tears): Well, I et all the cookies which you ain't s'posed to and then I got sick and frew up and then I had to be punished.

YOU: Oh Wow! So how do you feel now?

TILLIE (checking to be sure Mommy's not nearby): Well—it was worth it!

The flip side of the OK Kid is the **Not OK Kid** or **−Child**, full of hurt, of fear and guilt, anger and hostility, demanding and placating (manipulative), sadistic and vengeful, or masochistic. This is what explains the seemingly senseless destruction seen in school vandalism, the cruelty of some children toward others, the taunting and name calling. As grownups, these Not OK Kids continue on with spouse or child abuse, sexism, racism, and all the varieties of bigotry, subtle and direct. NONVERBAL CLUES: Angry flush (redfaced); quivering lip; downcast eyes; soft, quaky voice; pouting or whining; temper tantrums; throwing things; violent acting-out or hitting; jealousy and selfishness; defiance. VERBAL CLUES: "I'm scared! I can't. No! I won't. I'll show you. You're dumb/ugly. Gimme, it's mine. Please?"

EXERCISE 23

Think of something you should be doing in your everyday life, a habit you need to control (smoking, eating, drinking?), some skill or ability you want to master (become a more scientific interviewer?). So why can't you do it? Ask yourself that pointed question. **That** is your Parent!

EXERCISE 24

Think of a happy childhood memory, something you did as a child that you really enjoy, that you'd still probably get a kick from. Remember happy times such as Christmas, birthday parties, vacations. Dwell on it, feel good, be there again for a few moments. **That** is your OK Kid!

EXERCISE 25

If the world were divided into two countries, the **Nation of Thinking** and the **Nation of Feeling,** where would you live? The Thinkerpeople live where it's cold, at the North and South Poles, surrounded by clean, white snow, in gigantic ice castles. They do everything by computer because they believe in knowledge: "Knowledge is power; thinking is better than feeling." At the Equator, in the hot tropics, the Feelingpeople live in thatched huts. They don't wear any clothes or have any laws. They "go with the flow" and believe feeling is better than knowing: "If it feels good it *is* good." In such a world, most people live somewhere between these two countries. There's 70-30-ville and 40-60-ville. Where do you live? Think of yourself as a total person, the real you, and put a number to it on the thinking-feeling scale (90-10 would be 90 percent thinking and 10 percent feeling—unlikely). Self-analysis like this is done by your **Adult**.

Games

A **game** is a transaction (exchange of strokes) with a payoff, a bottom line, a hook, a scorpion's tail sting. A game ends with hurt feelings. If you "feel funny" while talking with someone, chances are you're in a game. Some games are very subtle and difficult to detect. Games are played at about a 4-year-old behavior level and most of them are unconscious, like the defense mechanisms described in the previous chapter. You should know about them to keep from getting caught up in them, to keep your eyes clear, your camera lens clean.

Picture yourself as a vertical arrangement of the three circles of P, A, and C (P on top, C on the bottom). If you have been able to get in touch with, to experience, your Parent, Adult, and Child by reading the descriptions above and by doing the last three exercises, you are in touch with the **real you.** Everything discussed in this book should have helped you see into yourself, strengths and weaknesses. Now picture a second column of P–A–C. That's the next person you're going to have contact with or the next person you interview or interrogate. Strokes are lines drawn from the circle or ego state giving the stroke to the circle of the ego state receiving the stroke. I say "hello" and you say "hello" back—that's two parallel lines from my Adult to yours. It's a harmless ritual of greeting. If you're in trouble with your boss, when he says "hello" it could be from his critical −Parent to your anxious −Child, you feel bad, and you're in a game called "kick me."

Some couples battle each other with verbal put downs, innuendo, and insult. These come from the Parent and are arrows shot at the −Child of the other person. If I shoot from my Parent to your Child and you do the same, the lines of the transaction are crossed, just like swords or crossed wires. Whenever you have crossed lines you are in conflict. People who yell at each other play a game called **Uproar** and those like you and me who are more sophisticated play **Museum** or **Archaeology,** the winner being the person with the best memory of previous hurts and insults. Here's Uproar:

HE (slamming door): I'm here.

SHE: So I **hear.** Can't you make more noise?

HE (raising voice): Not as well as you, foghorn!

SHE (also with raised voice): Look who the hell's talking!

HE (more volume): I got a big loudspeaker to compete with.

SHE (in a shriek): Well let's tell the world!

Nobody would buy it as a movie script. It's a waste of time and energy, but that's how most domestic arguments sound if you could write them down. Here's Museum:

HE: You really hurt my feelings by not asking me before you bought the new dishes.

SHE: Last time I asked you, last week, about getting the TV fixed, you said no.

HE: I was irritated then because the month before you didn't want to talk about trading in the stereo.

SHE: Sure, that was because last Christmas you wouldn't agree to buy new tires, just before I had a flat at rush hour downtown.

HE: Well, what we needed was a new car and the summer before you didn't want to hear about it.

This is the same game, but played with less force. The person with the best memory wins. With Olympic class players, the last line would probably be: "You screwed up before you were born!" These direct confrontation games are easy to recognize. Many games are more subtle and are called **hidden** or **duplex** because they're not what they appear to be. Here's one that sounds like it's Adult-to-Adult. As you read it, try to figure out what's **really** happening.

ME: I got a problem and I need your help. I'm getting to work late and the boss sees me.

YOU: Why not get a clock radio and wake up earlier with nice, restful music?

ME: Yes, but I have a clock radio, only it doesn't work and I don't know who could fix it.

YOU: I know a place on the way to work. You could drop it off on the way.

ME: Yes, but I don't have the money right now. I won't borrow from friends.

YOU: OK, I'll phone you in the morning when I get up.

ME: Yes, but I don't believe in imposing on friends.

YOU: Why don't you get a neighbor to knock on your door in the morning?

ME: Yes, but I don't want my neighbors to know my problems.

YOU: Dammit, you *really do* have a problem!

ME: Yes, it's just like a said! Woe is me!!

This was not Adult-to-Adult at all, but a hidden transaction between my Not OK Kid and your critical –Parent. I provoked you into moving from your Adult, where you began, to the judgmental –Parent. I moved down from my Adult (if I was ever there) to my Not OK Kid for a **kick me** payoff, and you eventually obliged. My masochistic Not OK Kid wanted a beating. This game is called **Yes, but.** Many substance abusers use it so they can continue to suffer and relieve the suffering with alcohol or drugs.

Here's another. You and your spouse save your money for several years to buy a very special oriental rug. It's a rainy day when the rug is carefully placed by experts (at extra cost) and you come home in a rush and track mud over it. Spouse doesn't even glare. In fact, you're a bit confused that there isn't a game of Uproar, or at least some Museum. Even more confusing, days pass and nothing is ever mentioned. Then, on the weekend, the President of the United States is visiting in your area and has a sudden need to go to the bathroom. The Secret Service choose your home for this emergency Presidential service. After "answering nature's call," the President agrees to sit and relax a moment in your living room and chat with the two of you:

SPOUSE: Mr. President, what do you think of this carpet?

PRESIDENT: It's a very beautiful carpet.

SPOUSE: Mr. President, we saved five years to buy it.

PRESIDENT: Yes, I can see it's expensive.

SPOUSE: There is no other carpet like it in the world.

PRESIDENT: It looks rare and very special.

SPOUSE: It is so special it took seven workers five hours just to put it there.

PRESIDENT: A very, very special, beautiful carpet indeed.

SPOUSE (now looking directly at you with the **gallows transaction** icy stare): Mr. President, what would you think of a person who, knowing how expensive and rare it is, the cost of having it installed, and the need to take special care of it, tracked mud over it the first day it was put down?

Bingo! You've had it. A set-up, build-up, and bear trap climax, hooked, hounded, and hung in a game called **NIGYSOB**, for "now I've got you, you son-of-a-bitch." Some game players add an extra step for added effect. If the President replied, "I consider such a person to be the lowliest creature in the universe," or some similar devastating comment, spouse continues the icy stare and says: "Sweetheart, would you know anyone like that?" That game is a variation of NIGYSOB called **Sweetheart**. Games can be mild, like playful teasing put-downs. These are called **first degree** games. A game that ends with a more forceful psychological or emotional "push" of hurt feelings, rejection, disappointment, or frustration is a **second degree game**. Substance abuse, child and spouse abuse, divorce, mental illness, and suicide are payoffs of **third degree games**.

EXERCISE 26

Think back about a conversation you have had recently in which you felt very uncomfortable. Could it have been a game? Chart the transaction with your PAC and the PAC of the other person. Was it a game? If so, will you now be more aware of how it started? What can you do next time? Here are some suggestions:

Doc Mac's Snake Bite Kit

The antidote, the "snake oil" for these painful bites is to know the games or where the "fangs" are so that you don't unknowingly get bitten. To be forewarned is to be forearmed. The rule of thumb is that if you feel bad in a conversation, you're probably in a game. Other signs: games are usually repetitive, use deception or surprise, hidden agendas, are not Adult at all. To complete Doc Mac's snake bite kit: Don't start games and if you're in a game, stop playing by moving into your Adult. If you can't get out of a game quickly, **stay in your Adult** and **center** and **ground yourself** as described earlier in this chapter. Every time you center yourself in your Adult you give yourself an inoculation against gamebite! Your Adult is the only part of you that can see all three ego states of others and at the same time be in touch with all three of your own. That's 20-20 vision for what's happening. The Adult is flexible, in touch with reality more than your Parent or Child, considers and chooses alternatives, what to say and do next, and can lead you out of the jungle games players like to stalk you through.

Scripts, Life Positions, Injunctions

Some people specialize in the games they play. There is a pattern to their game playing. It is as if they were actors and actresses following a **script**. In a sense, we all have scripts—life goals, plans, hopes, and aspirations. If your real-life family comes from a long line of doctors, lawyers, teachers, law enforcement, blue collar, or white collar workers, you may have been handed a **family** script. Male chauvinism, fem lib, racism, politics, and religion can also be scripted. If you can see and be your **real self**, there is little danger from scripts. To follow any script robot-like, without realizing your own individual needs, wishes, and values makes it more difficult for you to see not only who you are, but also others—your camera lens is tinted.

EXERCISE 27

This is an optional exercise to help you find and examine your life script. Who named you (what's in/behind your name)? Who are your heroes/heroines? What's your: favorite movie, movie star, book, fairy tale, poem? What was usually discussed during meals, throughout your childhood? How does your family react to stress? What's their attitude about religion, politics, your job, marriage, hobbies, habits? What feelings bother you the most? Are you the same as they, different or a mixture? Is that OK?

There are four basic **life positions** from which scripts can develop: **I'm NOT OK but you're OK** is the universal position of infancy and early childhood, when we are totally dependent on others; **I'm OK but you're not OK** is the battered child or spouse, innocent but punished anyway; **I'm NOT OK and you're NOT OK** is depression, despair, hopelessness; **I'm OK; you're OK** is the ideal, Adult-to-Adult relationship where the OK Kids are let out to play and Parents help build a better society. From time to time, you will find yourself feeling as if you are in one of these four life positions. It's normal for a short time, and hopefully you will begin and end in the I'm OK you're OK position. Those you interview and interrogate will be in one of these positions.

Parental injunctions are verbal and nonverbal messages or judgments of you which you receive from infancy. They can become part of your —Parent tape and life script. You will see them in persons you interview or interrogate:

1. **Don't be.** Don't exist. This is the unwanted child, feeling unwanted: "We really didn't want you, Hezekiah, but we love you just the same" or "I was in labor three days and three nights, almost died, and couldn't have any more kids, but it's OK."

2. **Don't grow up** (always be my kid). As old as you are, when you visit parents you're always a kid. Some women get the cold shoulder from Dad as childhood ends, and Mom weeps at the wedding because her "baby" is leaving. Some widows/widowers symbolize son or daughter as the dead spouse and make it difficult for them to lead their own lives.

3. **Don't be a child,** grow up! This is the "only child" trap often denied sharing with playmates and siblings and "growing up" too soon. If parents fight, the only child may feel somehow responsible. You're hugged like a baby when sick but told to "be brave and grownup" for painful injections.

4. **Don't be well,** depend on me! When Little Leroy is sick, Mom makes chicken soup and Dad reads him stories. Shy Sheilah has epilepsy but her parents discourage her going out to play with other kids. Jim has a "weak heart" and he stays home, too, where he gets a birthday cake every week (!) and ice cream every day.

5. **Don't be you,** be who I like/want/need. "Pretty Pam, we really wanted a boy but we still love you." This one surfaces in names (Martina for Martin) and Johnny Cash's song **A boy named Sue** pokes fun at this practice.

6. **Don't be important,** don't achieve. Some women raised in a sexist environment get the message they are not as good as men despite abilities and strengths. Men of lower intelligence in a home of professionals may not strive to use real abilities in areas of strength.

7. **Don't make it**—fail so I can take care of you. This is the overprotective parent who may talk about and pay for education or training but resent it because the child gets what the parent never

had. The victim often does well initially but fails to satisfy this injunction.

8. **Don't feel.** This is a denial of feelings and their significance. Little Lucy falls off the swing and Daddy says: "It doesn't hurt." But it does! Parents uncomfortable with their own feelings often discount them and children learn that feelings aren't important.

9. **Don't think.** Similar to don't feel, this one tells children thinking too much is not a good thing. It's better to remain stupid, then someone will take care of you, will think for you. A slave mentality.

10. **Don't own (or like) your body.** Be ashamed of it. Tall people who slouch, those who cover up their bodies, avoid swimming, dancing, and informal socializing because of real or imagined physical or personal defects.

11. **Don't belong.** You're different—better or worse. "Stick to your own kind," as sung in **West Side Story**. Can be based on differences of race, religion, ethnicity, social status or income, neighborhood, region, politics, or occupation.

12. **Just plain DON'T!** Don't "rock the boat" in any way. Vegetate in neutral. Try and you lose and that hurts. Come back into the hot tub of life where it feels good, or if bad it's still better than failure, pain, and death. This is a message delivered by fearful, overprotective parents.

Counterinjunctions are short automatic "must" messages that play in your head that reinforce or contradict parental injunctions. Some of the more common ones: "Mind your own business, don't air dirty linen; always work hard, go the extra mile, show'em what you can do; don't be naughty or bad, but be nice, good; get all A's; never tell a lie."

Miniscript drivers are also short "must" messages called **drivers** because they're like little motors running at idle, engaged by everyday events in your life which shift them from neutral to high, such as a someone's question or comment, an interruption, even a phone ringing or a bill or letter in the mail. There are five **drivers** and you have 'em all:

I would be OK if only I: **try harder**
                       hurry up
                       was strong
                       was perfect
                       pleased him/her/them/me

Most people use one or two of these drivers more than others. Knowing your usual drivers will help you cope with them and prevent them from getting in your way as you question others. It may sound childish, but the best way to neutralize these pesky automatic messages is to **memorize** a specific antidote for each. These, called **allowers,** will play back as automatically as the driver. Try typing allowers on an index card and putting it at your telephone. If you're doing something important and the phone rings, you have a few seconds during the first three rings to read the short allower message.

If your **driver** is that you must:	. . . then your allower is: **It's OK to**
try harder	**do and not overdo**
hurry up	**take time**
be strong	**be myself**
be perfect	**make mistakes sometimes**
please me/others	**just be me**

EXERCISE 28

Review the parental injunctions, counterinjunctions, and miniscript drivers and list the ones that apply to you in one column. How many might get in your way when you question others? Select an antidote to neutralize each of them and a plan of corrective action. Follow that plan.

Structuring Time

Eric Berne described six ways we spend time together: **withdrawal, rituals, pastimes, activities, games,** and **intimacy.** Picture yourself sitting on an airliner headed for a 2-week vacation all by yourself. The stranger sitting next to you is very attractive. What a wonderful opportunity to "get acquainted." What potential excitement. Most people find it so scary they immediately invent ways to structure the situation. You can listen to everyday conversations and gauge distance between people and their comfort level by what is discussed. Doing this will help you develop your listening skills and your understanding of human nature. Let's tune in:

Withdrawal. This is the most distancing. It's going to a meeting or being in a group but sitting alone, into your own thoughts and feelings, not mixing in. Withdrawing can be caused by a Parent message ("better not; never know what'll happen!"), your Child ("this is awful scary; we might get hurt") or your Adult ("Hmmm. Let's analyze this situation. If we get involved . . . and if we don't . . . so . . . maybe . . . ").

Rituals are safe, predictable, less involved ways to relate to people. **Greeting** is a ritual. People meet and say "hello" (means only that you acknowledge someone's presence), "how are you?" (acknowledges them personally but you don't **really** want to know how they are), and "fine" (even if they feel awful) and "see you" or "take care" or the grand slam "have a nice day" (means you're returning on course on your way again). Sometimes the whole ritual is a quick exchange of: "Hi!" Nonverbal rituals can be mandatory **loose** handshakes and **empty** hugs. Sex, work, hobbies, even birthday and other parties can become rituals. Nothing's **really** happening. That's the idea.

Pastimes are more personal than rituals, a few degrees warmer and deeper, but not much. There are men, women, and mixed pastimes. Examples of men pastimes: cars, sports, women, war, job, and handyman. Women pastimes: kitchen, wardrobe, home, families, and men. Mixed pastimes: weather (always a safe subject), food, travel ("ever been to . . . "), people ("whatever happened to . . . "), children ("guess what Johnny did"), aging ("when I was a kid") and current events. This is about as far as most coworkers, friends, neighbors, club and church members go in conversation. Even controversial subjects can be pastimed and thus made safe, such as discussing comparative religion in a church group, politics among party activists, AIDS or sex education at a PTA meeting.

Activities take time and can be done in a group, such as work, sports, clubs, and hobbies, or alone, like restoring furniture, renovating the house, repairing the car, or a solitary hobby. Activities can be used to avoid close contact (alone in the basement doing fix-it) or to win warm fuzzies ("My, what a wonderful job! And you did it all by yourself").

Games have already been described, transactions with a win-lose payoff. They take time and they also avoid close, deep relationships. They do not bring people together, but push them apart, or down.

Intimacy is game-free sharing agreed to (not **a greed** to either of us), appropriate, accepted, mutually supportive, never exploitive. It's free, direct, usually warm and sincere uninhibited 50-50 "straight talk" communication between two people who trust and are open to each other. It's the "buddy system" where your life can depend on the other person, both of you know and accept it, and feel good about it because you trust each other. Intimacy can be between two trusted friends, coworkers, spouses, or family members, adult to child or child to child. People who share TA intimacy are not interested in and are incapable of playing games. Intimacy is the ideal relationship.

WHAT HAVE YOU LEARNED?

This chapter divided human interaction into two parts: **nonverbal behaviors** and **verbal behaviors**. Where you are and what you and others do physically has as much impact as what is said. Nonverbal behaviors were studied in terms of place, mental space, and psychological distance, time and timing, costumes, ornamentation, and props, role behavior, body placement and posture, and movement and mannerisms of body parts most used in verbal communication, facial expression, masks, and head movement, touch, and involuntary signs of underlying stress from the autonomic nervous system. A system of shorthand notations for 20 body parts was described which can be used to record nonverbal behaviors when they occur.

Verbal behaviors were explored according to transactional analysis theory. Strokes (warm, cold, plastic) and their exchange as transactions were studied as functions of the three P–A–C ego states (Parent, Adult, Child). Games, transactions with a painful payoff, were described with "Doc Mac's snakebite kit" to prevent getting enmeshed in games. Scripts, life positions, counterinjunctions, and miniscript drivers were then discussed with suggestions for their neutralization and control.

If you are familiar with these ideas, have done all the exercises in this chapter to apply them to yourself, and have observed nonverbal and verbal behaviors you will better understand the persons you will question in interview or interrogation. You are ready to put this and the two preceding chapters together and apply all these learnings to interview and interrogation settings. If not, please go back and reread and review the content. If you are interested in transactional analysis and want to read more, here is a recent reference and a good overview of the entire field. It includes concepts introduced after Berne and Harris and many self-awareness exercises:

Stewart, I., & Joines, V. *TA today: A new introduction to transactional analysis.* Chapel Hill, NC: Lifespace Publishing, 103 Edwards Ridge, Chapel Hill, NC 27514.

Sources for additional information on nonverbal behavior are these articles:

Ekman, P., Friesen, V., & Bear, J. (1984): The international language of gestures. *Psychology Today, 18* (May 1984), pages 64–69.
Ekman, P., & Oster, H. (1978). Facial expressions of emotion. *Annual Review of Psychology, 30,* 527–554.

Chapter 4

INTERVIEW

> "When I use a word," Humpty Dumpty
> said, in rather a scornful tone, "it means
> just what I choose it to mean, neither
> more nor less"
> Lewis Carroll
> *(Through the Looking Glass)*

Interview or Interrogation?

Interviews **collect information** to reach a **conclusion.** Interrogation **recreates and documents an event** to **get and confirm evidence** or **indepth information on a specific subject.** An effective interview can be done in an hour or less, but Interrogation in most cases takes hours and may require several sessions. Good interrogators are good interviewers but good interviewers may lack the skill necessary to interrogate well. This is due not just to the shorter time, less depth, less detail for interviewing, and less of an adversarial relationship—most people who are interrogated have reason to avoid telling the truth. Detecting deception and seeing "through" people is a skill that requires a higher degree of knowledge and training. Other comparisons:

INTERVIEW	INTERROGATION
Light	Heavy
More general	More specific
Social level	Psychological-emotional
Peruse, review	Probe, research
Take notes	Tape it
Hour or less	More than an hour
News article	Investigative reporting
Brochure	Book
Painting, sketch	Detailed photograph

Mirror, window	Microscope, telescope
Flashlight	Floodlight

Whether for employment, performance appraisal, a credit purchase, magazine or newspaper article, polls or research, military or industrial intelligence, military debriefings, or to interview a crime victim or witness, all interviews share the common goal of getting information. They are conversations in motion, going somewhere, in a definite direction, and the interviewer is the pilot. To be effective, interviews should be **scientific,** conducted as closely as possible according to the **scientific method** described in Chapter 1.

The Interview Process

Planning. You should spend at least as much time to prepare for an interview as actually conducting it. You need a written list of what it is you need to know, the information you are seeking. Review the list to ensure it is complete. Review it again and rearrange questions so that "easy" questions of relatively trivial value or least emotional discomfort begin the interview. You want a smooth flow into the "meat." "Salt in" the "hard" or probing questions. Now take a good, l-o-n-g look at them to plan your overall strategy. Interviewing should be like a stage play, movie, or piece of music, with a smooth opening, good development (of information), returning to a smooth ending. You should use **word economy,** concise journalistic style. Being too wordy can mislead and confuse or make an already uncomfortable process much more upsetting. Being too brief can be received as uncaring and abrupt. Finally, you should know as much about the persons to be questioned as possible, to cancel out any bias you might have, and to better understand them.

Preparation. Before any questions are asked, the person to be interviewed should be prepared for what is to follow. This is **informed consent,** the equivalent to reading so-called "Miranda rights" to a suspect charged with a crime. It starts with meeting the victim or witness. You should be aware of your own nonverbal and verbal behaviors. Your personal appearance should reflect neatness and good grooming. You should **take time** to introduce yourself, with a relatively slow handshake (loosened up for women), and a reassuring tone of voice. First impressions **are** important and you can greatly facilitate the flow of information by establishing trust and rapport as soon as possible. Avoid standing around. Lead them into the interview room.

Interview rooms should be "homey" and comfortable. Even if there is a zero budget, it is possible to get curtains, carpet, and room furnishings from staff who are discarding these from home. If this doesn't work, try the Salvation Army Thrift Store or Goodwill Industries. A can of paint costs little. The effect on interview effectiveness is well worth it. Interview rooms should NOT look like they're in a police station, government office, or hospital. They should be informal and comfortable. A table may help you take notes, but it can also be an obstacle between you and your source of information. Try substituting a clipboard if you need a writing surface. It's best to let the person choose his or her own chair since the chairs are equally placed. You should sit down after them, neither too close nor too far away. The physical distance between you should allow for a slightly lower volume than social conversation enough to be heard. Every interview room should have a sign outside that reads INTERVIEW IN PROGRESS and slides or flips over to read ROOM VACANT. Ensure you are not disturbed. Interruptions interfere with your concentration and that of the person being questioned, waste time, stop the flow of conversation, increase psychological distance, and prove Murphy's Law, occurring at the worst possible time.

You should keep your own talk at a minimum, getting the interviewee to "give" more. For crime victims, it's best to begin in a reassuring voice, apologizing for the need to again go into details of what is a disturbing event. Witnesses should be thanked for their time and interest and complimented for doing their duty as a citizen. Military debriefing is also a time for expressing thanks for their time and interest and a word about the need for and the value of the information. Employment interviews and performance appraisals should begin much the same, with an explanation of the need to meet. These courtesies are not recommended because they are good public relations but because doing so facilitates the interview process, makes for better results. They "break the ice," set the tone, and ensure entry into the questioning phase smoothly and with a minimum of resistance or hypersensitivity.

Performance. If you can imagine the interview process as a sandwich, the **performance** step is the meat. Planning and presentation are the bread and lettuce. Performance is the "work" of the interview. In police work, it is to find out more about the crime and the criminal. In personnel work, it is to discover more about the prospective employee or his or her work for performance appraisal. In news reporting, it is to get a "story" or "scoop" of interest to the public. In military or industrial intelligence, get as much information as possible about the enemy or a competitor's operations. While all these applications occur in widely separated occupations and settings, the **process** and most interview techniques are the same and are described below. For most interviews, an informal, friendly atmosphere is best.

Product. This is the final result of interviewing. If all goes well, you have all the information you set out to collect, and hopefully more.

XYZ Communications Styles

Each of us has a typical conversational style, a basic approach to getting and processing information from others. The following are descriptions of three types of persons, X, Y, and Z. Read each one. Reread them if you wish. Which of the three best matches the **real you,** not how you want to be but how you are now. Which is the next most like you? The remaining person will be least like you. Write the letters in order starting with the person you are most like, then read the **key** which follows the descriptions.

Person X is task-oriented, likes details, is organized and systematic, careful and meticulous and strives for accuracy, likes to analyze, collect data and explore various possibilities and alternatives, usually keeps a neat desk, orderly files, and can find anything in them, is seen as reliable, fair, stable, a conscientious hard worker. NEEDS: Security and stability in a fair, just world where everything is predictable and orderly. PROBLEM AREAS: If you're an X, you're careful and like detail, and seldom get all the information you need and therefore tend to procrastinate and miss deadlines. Some see you as a nitpicker who gets bogged down in details and misses the big picture or overly cautious and resist change. You may not like to delegate because you know what has to be done and "if you want it done right you gotta do it yourself." Since few people are as careful and attentive to detail as you, you may be lonely. You would "rather be right than President." The "criminal X" is the planner or "mastermind."

Person Y is goal-oriented, wants to know "the bottom line," and asks "what's the purpose, the goal, the target?" Fast-paced, forceful, bold, quick on the trigger, "take charge" and "hands on" achiever, doer, and driver who is also driven from within, determined, decisive, ambitious, proud, and impulsive. NEEDS: Authority, status, and achievement, with new challenges and targets, "new worlds to conquer." PROBLEM AREAS:

If you're a Y, you are impatient and impulsive, some see you as insensitive, demanding, bossy, or reckless and "going off half cocked," and you may miss the small picture, the many details that can snare and trap you. Your behavior says: "Let's get the show on the road. It's already late. If you're not part of the solution, you're part of the problem. Move out. Let's go!" The "criminal Y" is the "hit man" or "gunman."

Person Z is people-oriented, accepting, compassionate, helpful, and supportive, a positive thinker, an optimist who likes to "talk it over" as an equal, sharing partner, who gets along well with people who don't get along with others and therefore is well liked, a peacemaker, forgiving, a good compromiser smoothing over ruffled feathers and troubled waters. NEEDS: People, acceptance, belonging, appreciation, freedom, and variety. PROBLEM AREAS: If you're a Z, being all things to all people causes you to be inconsistent and lack focus on goals, seen by some as overdoing the compromise, too emotional, wasting time, missing facts and the point. Your behavior says: "You gotta feel good to do good. Feelings are facts. Everybody should have a voice and a vote in everything that happens." The "criminal Z" is the "con artist."

Key
(Don't read until you've classified yourself as mostly Person X, Y or Z)

Person X is a "heavy" Adult in TA terms, an analytical accumulator of information constantly seeking more. Person Y is a "heavy" Parent in TA terms and an authoritative activator aimed at the bull's eye. Person Z is a "heavy" TA Child, compassionate and caring who needs people. In a war, Y would make an ideal military commander, X should be in charge of weapons production and research, and Z should manage all the personnel. Here's a further comparison:

X	Y	Z
Detailer	Authoritarian	Compassionate
Task-oriented	Goal-oriented	People-oriented
Analyzes	Directs	Compromises
Misses big picture	Misses details	Misses the point
Hands off, let's look	Hands on, do it!	Let's hold hands!

Each of us has all three of these qualities, but most of us have one more than others. Some have a tie for first or second place but rarely an even three-way split among X, Y, and Z. For interviewing and interrogating there is but one ideal "home base" and that's X. In fact X is the secret ingredient that can make the difference between a mediocre questioner and an expert. Of course, as in all human behavior, extremes should be avoided. Too much X would drown you in a sea of minutia. The three qualities should be in dynamic balance with X clearly in control for effective interview and interrogation. Y too "bull in a China shop" impulsive and may miss valuable verbal and nonverbal clues. Z is too "touchy feely" and tends to give people the benefit of the doubt. On the other hand, some good fictional detectives come in all three packages: Sherlock Holmes, an inquisitive, skilled X; Kojak, a brash Y; Columbo, a perceptive but people-oriented old shoe of a Z. If you are predominantly Y or Z, you should work at being more X when interviewing and interrogating. It will save you time and trouble. Keep Y and Z secondary. You need Y to keep you on track and Z to know when to let go and not bulldoze over people.

EXERCISE 29

Are you basically an X, Y, or Z type interviewer? What are the disadvantages to using only that approach in your questioning? How can you weave in the other two for a good balance? Develop a plan to do this. Arrange with a coworker to help you practice a better balance and give you feedback about it.

Interview Do's and Don'ts

There are eight major guidelines to **scientific** interviewing, three don'ts and five do's:

1. **Don't Overload** by asking several questions at once, using complex sentences with many parts, "either or" choices, or questions within questions, unless you intend to. Doing so makes for shorter answers, of less depth (and so, incomplete information), and can confuse the person interviewed. The best interview moves step by step, drop by drop, not bucket by bucket.

2. **Don't Lose Control of the Interview.** If **you** are not in control of the interview, who is? If you ramble or the person interviewed goes off on tangents, you can lose your place in your interview strategy. If

you allow or encourage overanswering you waste time. It is good technique to allow some of this because it can add to the information database but not if it is not relevant or useful at all and is only an ego trip for you or the interviewed. Other ways of losing control: **preaching, teaching,** or **selling.** Interviews are not for these purposes. Be a listener, not a lecturer, a receiver not a transmitter, but **do** be a clockwatcher.

3. **Don't Lose Your Focus** by rephrasing answers in your own words. Always use the words and phrases of the person interviewed. If you use your own, you are subtly reframing and shaping the interview. If unchecked you will hear what the interviewed person thinks you want to hear. This can be entirely inadvertent or a conscious effort to deceive. The interview can become a mutual admiration society discussing self-fulfilling prophecies and truths. Effective interviewers give little or nothing and get everything they need. Be a sponge, not the soap!

4. **Do Be Alert, Fully Aware, and Carefully Attentive.** Know what's happening, what is likely to happen, and what already happened. See what's there, not what you want to see or expect to see. Let the truth emerge of and by itself. You are a midwife, an interpreter, a skilled observer and reporter.

5. **Do Break the Ice, Set an Open, Receptive Atmosphere.** Greet cordially, be courteous and respectful, ensure everyone is comfortable. Always start loose and tighten up as needed. Loose openers: weather, local or national sports or current event, where's the restroom, nearby place for lunch—anything of interest **not** at all related to the interview.

6. **Do Follow Your Map,** your **overall** strategic plan to get all the information you need. This is best done in small steps. As the Chinese philosopher LaoTse said 2500 years ago, "the journey of a thousand miles starts with the first step." It is like stringing beads to make a beautiful necklace. You may and probably will be side-tracked from time to time on side roads. You may even do this yourself, if it helps gain needed information, but you must always return to the main road and continue the journey.

7. **Do Be Flexible,** like a ship, able to increase or decrease speed, reverse, or move according to the weather and current of the interview as it develops. This may sound like a contradiction to the above commandment, but the key word there is to follow and

always return to your **overall** strategy. If you are too rigid and hold **too** closely to strategy, you can miss valuable information not known before interview and which you won't be aware of during the interview. Be open, not closed, receptive to new information, but with the big picture, your goal and strategy, in sharp focus.

8. **Do Know When to Stop.** When you have the information you need, hopefully a bit more, it's time to close shop. The rule is "get it and get out." I call it the "kissoff." End as you began, with thanks for their time, interest, and cooperation, how useful the information will be. Walk them to the door and assist with any additional information. If a crime victim or witness interview, be certain you give them a phone number and several names of persons to call with any additional information.

Special Applications

Crime, News, Military or Industrial Intelligence

Crime victims and witnesses are interviewed to obtain a detailed description of the criminal and the crime. In news reporting, military debriefing, and military and industrial intelligence, the goal is to accumulate as much accurate, useful information as possible. The quest for information is the goal of all interview situations. The information needed is in the mind and memory of the person being questioned. Memory is far more easily used than explained. Just as for personality and intelligence, there is no definition of memory accepted by all researchers or theorists in the field. There is, however, a growing consensus that memory consists of two or more separate but interrelated systems (Tulving, 1985). One of these systems is based on association or stimulus-response connections, a kind of "learning by doing" or "knowing how" from actual, direct life experience. It is memory as in the old saying: "Experience is the best teacher." That kind of learning is imbedded deeply in this memory bank. Another memory system is based not on actual experience but on deductions or ideas from previous experience, on visualization or representation, an "as if" or "knowing about" memory. There may be more memory systems than these two. No one has been able to find a "memory center" in the brain despite decades of hard laboratory research. Some researchers believe memory is more a process than a system (Denton, 1988).

Difficulty recalling factual information about an event can increase when that event is a crime because of psychological and emotional stress. Research studies show that victim and witness testimony can be mistaken. Hypnosis research tells us memory can be permanently and erroneously altered by being hypnotized (MacHovec, 1986). Polygraph (lie detector) and sodium amytal (truth serum) interviews can be faked. These are clear warning signs to anyone conducting interviews to proceed with extreme caution, to take special care to obtain factual information without misleading questions. The following 7-step process steps are recommended:

1. **Mining.** This is obtaining the raw material or first answers with simple, brief, open-ended questions such as: "Tell me in your own words what you saw on April 12, 1989 at or about 11:00 PM." At this stage, do NOT interrupt or ask more specific questions. Avoid words of reassurance. Wait out the pauses. Take notes or record responses. You are **mining,** that's all. To do anything more is to risk contaminating the memory bank. Many interviewers limit notes to the left side of the letter-sized page, and triple spaced. You'll soon see why. This first step serves as an "ice breaker" and "tunes in" memory to specific time limits and place.

2. **Refining.** ONLY when the raw material stage (above) is complete do you yourself take a more active part in the interview. You now ask to go over the event again, this time in detail. It is at this stage you ask specific questions, focus on details. Most poor interviewers move too quickly here. Take your time, get it all. Too much evidence, too many leads are lost here. These notes fill in the spaces in the left hand column of your notes. You're refining what you mined! It taps the factual recall system of memory.

   Memory can be refreshed **directly** or **indirectly.** Direct recall is **free** when the person tries to remember without help, and **cued** when someone asks specific questions to help refresh memory. Indirect recall is to "creep up" tangentially on memory, by thinking about other events somehow similar. Example: If you lost your dog, imagine you **are** the dog. Where could you be? This works as well with list objects (keys, wallet, etc.). Another indirect method is to deliberately **not** try to remember. Often, the memory just seems to "pop up." Word association and sentence completion tests indirectly lead the person to the event to be remembered. Be careful with your choice and use of words. It is important **not** to lead a crime victim or witness or job applicant by providing detail. Example: It is better to ask if the suspect was carrying anything, not "did he have a gun?" Ask about the **vehicle** not **the silver sports car**, what were the **circumstances** of changing jobs not "why were you fired?" **Never** use **value describer words** like **speeding** car, **drunk** driver.

3. **Retrogression.** This the single most important part of effective interviewing. At this stage you proceed **backward** from the most recent memory to the event. Start at the last entry in your notes and use the right-hand column. This taps the memory bank from the opposite direction and has yielded much valuable information. You now (and **only** now) have a good enough picture of what most likely occurred to proceed further. This step more deeply probes factual recall.

4. **Cross-Section.** These are like cross-sectional slices or test corings of ore, specific questions about the event to clarify certain facts. Poor interviewers barge in and ask these questions without the mining, refining, and retrogress steps above and run the risk of contaminating memory and, worse still, leading and shaping answers. This step provides quick, deep thrusts into important areas and is less stressful on the victim or witness since you can clarify painful subjects briefly, minimizing the pain of recall.

5. **Reliving.** This step can be done by returning to the scene. It should be audio-recorded because the victim or witness may say something seemingly trivial which can lead to valuable evidence, or something which contradicts previous statements. It is helpful to reenact the event exactly where it occurred. If it is not possible or practical to return to the scene, do this step in a quiet room with minimal distractions, comfortable furniture and allow enough time for emotional venting. This step facilitates the visualization memory system. Have a mental health professional available if there's a possibility the victim or witness will be agitated. If you have sufficient information, this step can be omitted.

6. **Refocus.** This optional step is a role play of the event which can be integrated into the previous step. It helps with visualization and factual recall. When victims have taken the criminal's part they have recalled more details of what was said and done.

7. **Review and Conclusions.** In this step, you read over, study, and reflect what you have accumulated, play back the tape (several

times), then go over with the victim or witness the transcript for refreshed memories stimulated by this review. ALWAYS leave your name and phone number with them and ask if there is anything else they would like to add—a last shot at additional memories.

EXERCISE 30

With a coworker or classmate studying this book, or by agreement with a family member or friend, choose an everyday event, such as the last time they went food shopping or to a store to make a purchase. Go through the seven steps listed above to recreate this event. Give and get feedback as to your interview style, positive and negative aspects. If a paired activity, let your partner question you about an event in your everyday life experience. It may be helpful to repeat this exercise after you have finished this book.

Uncooperative Witnesses. Occasionally, crime victims and witnesses do not cooperate in the interview process. There are several reasons for this. **Fear** is a common factor, with many facets. There can be a fear of publicity and its effect (embarrassment, more emotional pain, reputation, reprisal). If the witness implicates a supervisor, there can be a fear for job security. A child in a sexual abuse case may fear being removed from home or being blamed for the abuse. It may be simple avoidance of inconvenience and discomfort just by getting involved. They may feel a need to protect others, the criminal if somehow seen as similar, or to protect the victim from more pain. They may themselves have something to hide, perhaps a similar offense in the past. The witness may in fact be the offender! Typical behaviors of uncooperative witnesses: one-word answers, incomplete answers or "under-answering," being deliberately misleading (overanswering with useless or wrong information), volunteering nothing, flat refusal to answer, many pauses, looking down or away, being shy, inhibited or fearful, antagonistic, sarcastic, or hostile or hiding behind a smoke screen of humor. These behaviors can be the person's normal conversational style under stress, but they should still trigger your mental flashing red light for further study.

Countermeasures for uncooperative witnesses include reassurance for those motivated by fear and whichever of these is most appropriate: **right thing to do (duty)** with comments such as "you'll feel better for helping, and if you don't you'll probably feel guilty that you didn't do the right thing"; **revenge** ("You can make the difference. You can give us the information we need to prevent this from happening again"); **consequences** ("If you don't help us, it means someone else will be the victim, maybe someone you know, someone you love"). If witnesses share fear of reprisal they should be assured of protection. The least you can do is provide them with a phone number and several names, not just yours. If the case is serious and the witness testimony critical, special protection should be provided.

Cult Crime and Ritual Abuse

There is an organized nationwide movement of Satanic and other cults as well as part-time "dabblers" in the occult. Some engage in church and cemetery vandalism; child physical and sexual abuse; ritualistic sexual behavior; animal, fowl, and human mutilation; kidnapping; and murder. They indulge in bizarre practices such as bloodletting, smearing feces and blood on victims, eating feces, drinking urine, and placing small children inside the dismembered bodies of animals or in coffins with corpses for rebirthing. Rituals usually occur 1 AM to 3 AM, on Sunday morning and there are special holidays: January 1, 7 and 20; February 2 and 25; March 1 and 20; April 24 through 31; May 1; June 21 and 23; July 1 and 25; August 1, 3 and 24; September 7, 20 and 22; October 29 and 31; November 1 and 4; December 21, 22 and 24, and any 13th or 31st day of the month. Christmas, the birth of a baby (Jesus) is reversed to celebrate the death of an infant sacrifice. Reversed values are a clue to Satanic cult ritual.

Crime scenes with evidence of cult rituals would have no blood (it's been used), drawings or symbols (pentagram, 666, inverted cross, goat head, or OTO, etc.), goblets, a coffin, altar, 6-foot rope, "bone bag" with finger or other human bones, candles or dripped wax in a pattern, skulls, or colored robes. Children as young as 4 are spun, thrown, repeatedly violated physically and sexually, then locked away alone. Victims who speak of any of these practices or objects should be questioned further and referred for professional help. Frequently, they have multiple personality disorder, posttraumatic stress disorder, panic disorder, or phobias. Anyone charged with trespassing, vandalism, cruelty to animals, kidnapping, child abuse, or murder, where the crime scene shows any of these unusual clues, should be questioned more closely as they may be cult members.

Job Interviews

Research on personnel selection shows that reading applications beforehand increases the amount of correct information obtained in interview (Hakel, 1986). An important often missed factor in screening and interviewing job applicants is **resume analysis** and **evaluating applications.** Most applicants list information to present themselves in the best light. This information should be carefully reviewed **before** interview to create the best questions to separate fact from exaggeration. Example: Authorship of a book is listed which during interview is found to be an incomplete manuscript never reviewed by any publisher, or a published article is claimed only to discover it was coauthored by several people, the applicant **not** one of the major contributors. On the other hand, there can be references to exceptional performance (consistent promotions; authoring policy manuals, managing a department which set standards, sales or production records) and extras such as offices in organizations, chairing committees, giving speeches, honors, awards, volunteer work, or civic, service, church or fraternal memberships and activities.

On the negative side, here are loopholes to be questioned: **gaps** in job history; **salary differences** where income **decreased** progressively rather than increased; **diminished responsibility** in the same or succeeding jobs. These may be due to absenteeism, continuing substance abuse, even time out to serve time in jail. The less experienced tend to overstate education; the less educated stress experience. You must feel for the balance, to judge what is the best blend of both. Those who change jobs frequently may have unrealistic goals, personal problems, or be bored but gifted achievers looking for new worlds to conquer. You must see through the moving around and find the meaning. Less detail can mean few achievements or too few opportunities, another judgment call for you. Seeing "through" resumes and applications requires good interview skills, your own self-awareness, understanding human nature, knowing the applicant, and the Zen third eye and ear. All this suggests that there's a lot of BS in applications and resumes—which does **not** mean the applicant has a bachelor's degree!

Job interviews should go beyond the routine factors of education, training, and experience. Those are already listed on the application and resume and are more quantitative than qualitative factors. Here are some recommended questions that are qualitative on subjects not on most applications and resumes:

1. What do you see as the ideal job for you? What are you looking for? What do you like to do?
2. What strengths would you bring to this job?
3. What are your weaknesses? What irritates you most on the job, any job?
4. What's your management/supervision/leadership style?
5. How do you like to be supervised? How do you react to criticism? Give an example.
6. We've been having some difficulty with _____. How do you feel you could help with this?
7. Summing it up briefly, why should we hire you?

EXERCISE 31

Get a copy of your own most recent job application and review it for the positive and negative features described above. How would you now interview someone who submitted an application like that?

Performance Evaluations

Few people like or look forward to performance evaluation. For most jobs, they are required annually. Most authorities agree this is not frequent enough. Performance evaluation should be ongoing, actually every day, with many informal contacts between supervisor and worker throughout the year. Then, quarterly, semiannual, or annual report forms merely reflect what has been happening, without the need for a once yearly psychological and emotional trial—which is what it is for all too many workers. Anxiety, fear, distrust, and anger fester and ferment with distance in time or space and are relieved with closer, more frequent contact. The Jamestown settlers got along better with Indians living nearby than General Custer just "passing through" the Little Big Horn. U.S.-Soviet relations have improved since World War II to a large extent because the world has shrunk in travel time, technological access, and the view from outer space. As the song goes: "It's a small world after all."

Performance evaluation is a communications bridge that needs frequent traffic to function well. It is also an opportunity to vent feelings, prevent buildup of fear or frustration, clarify misunderstandings and differing expectations, and in these ways reduce turnover. Your goal as a performance evaluator is to find a middle ground on the communications bridge, and use it to review the past and plan the future. Done positively, it is a sharing of mutual satisfaction at what was done well, concerns and expectations at what wasn't, and shared expectations for the future. Here are three guidelines to help you achieve this goal:

1. **Open Up.** Develop and use an open, sincere, sharing attitude and atmosphere. State the goal (described above) and ask them for their help in achieving it. Doing so extends your hand as an equal sharing team member. Another way to reflect a sharing approach: "I wonder how you would like to see this review end. For me, I hope" (whatever you hope, or something like) "you and I can learn from the past and work together so that next year we can really feel good about what's happened." Poor technique: "So, it's my job to see what you did and didn't do." It may help if you **self-disclose**: "I always feel nervous and uncomfortable doing these" or "because I have to judge people." If you self-disclose, it's gotta be sincere and not play-acting.

2. **Funnel.** Move from loose, open style and content to more structured, specific job elements and performance. It's called the **funnel** because you move from the wide opening to specific tasks. Do this by direct reference to the specifics, by rephrasing what has been said in more detail, or use established or expected standards to reframe previous performance and what each of you expect mutually in the future to achieve goals. Poor technique: "Here's what you did wrong and what's gonna happen to you if you do it again."

3. **Be Positive.** This doesn't mean to ignore or minimize the negative. All negatives should be discussed, but not as sticks to use to beat better performance. Fear of punishment is not the best nor even a good way to improve performance. Criticism should **always** be based on **what** wasn't done according to standards, **never who** was responsible. In other words, it's **the work** that didn't get done and that's the need to be satisfied. If workers feel accepted as persons they can take a lot of criticism. Poor technique: "I guess I shouldn't have expected any more from **you**." Better technique: "Job 503 went so well I was really surprised this one didn't turn out the same way."

Everyone has strengths. Find them and use them in every performance evaluation. It's like these words from an old song: "You gotta accentuate the positive, eliminate the negative, and don't mess with Mister Inbetween." Example: If a worker complains more staff are needed to do a job, a positive reply could be: "Yes, I agree. But until we get more staff, what can we do to meet these targets?" I call this the **meanwhile back at ranch** approach.

The Stress Interview

In rare instances, a **stress interview** is used. The atmosphere is adversarial and stress is applied by an uncomfortable physical setting or questions asked in an unfriendly manner or in a coldly mechanical, monotonous "conveyor belt" repetition or by rapid fire "machine gun" delivery. Stress interviews attempt to move the person questioned off balance to outflank defenses and resistance. They seek to increase anxiety and fear. These emotions are powerful behavior modifiers. It doesn't take much effort to change the climate of an interview from one of acceptance to one of uncertainty and fear. Authority is power and power engenders fear in those without power. Interviewers schedule, open, conduct, and close the interview session. **That's** power.

Using fear can keep the person interviewed on edge, in self-defense, but the flip side is that this can cause defensiveness, making the whole interview process more difficult. Like using nuclear weapons, you have to know how much to use and when to stop. Experienced questioners do not use stress interviews, because the risk to the interview process is not worth the short-term advantage. If there were but one fact needed, this type of interview might be worth it. But in a cost-benefit analysis, stress interviews are generally not worth it. Pressure can be applied in interviews in a variety of ways. Here's one example: "Would you want this crime to happen to you or your family? He (or she) is loose on the street and we need the information you have to make an arrest." Or: "There's a killer on the street and I don't have time to be nice. Just answer the questions."

An example of how stress even with the best intentions can backfire is a case described by Mortimer Feinberg in an article in the *Wall Street Journal.* FBI Chief J. Edgar Hoover was a stickler for detail and a strict taskmaster. He insisted that all memos be no more than one page long, with wide margins. An agent violated this rule and Hoover wrote back: "Good analysis—watch the borders." FBI agents were rushed to the U.S.

and Mexican and Canadian borders. "Nobody knew what they were looking for," Feinberg reported, "but for a while, these borders were watched as never before" (1988).

Interview Interaction

Interviews can be like a warm bath or a cold shower, verbal massage or medieval torture. Interviews can motivate or they can alienate, push, or pull, join or separate you from those you interview. You set the stage and the pace. As discussed earlier, you should always center yourself in the TA Adult, but occasionally, consciously moving through Parent and Child gives you added flexibility and effectiveness and enables you to use a greater variety of interview techniques.

The ARC Method

Before any interview technique can be used effectively, you must brush up your skills in interacting with another person. The previous chapters have provided a good foundation, but now all that **knowledge** or "book larnin'" must be applied in practice. To be effective, every interaction should satisfy a 3-step process, the ARC method. Here it is:

A—Awake and Attentive!

The first step in any interaction is to **be there**. This means you must be alert and attentive, fully aware, observant, ready for whatever happens. That's the A stage, being **awake**. It also means **active attending** or **attentive listening**. You can be fully attentive but occasionally look up or away, out a window, at a picture, your pencil, the tabletop, the doorway. With good "side vision" you still won't miss anything. Practice this as you drive to and from work, at coffee break, when having chats with others. Notice what people wear, what's on the floor or ceiling, the many physical "things" we tend to miss. Notice, too, the words chosen, speed of delivery, tone of voice, loudness. Think about the mood they are likely to be in. If you know them well, after you've come to a tentative conclusion, **ask them**. This is an ideal opportunity, in a safe and neutral environment, to get feedback on the accuracy of your impressions. Hopefully, this book will have helped you be more objective and accurate. Be a blank slate, a camera with fresh, unused film, open, objective, ready.

R—Reflection, Mirroring

The second step is the one most people with communications problems miss. It's the **reflection** step, or **mirroring**. Most arguments between people could be prevented if everyone followed this second step in the ARC method. It requires that you first **understand** what is said **before** you react to it. It means you **never assume** anything. You reflect with opening statements such as: "I hear you saying" or "do you mean" or "are you saying" or the **Columbo:** "Let me see if I understand what you're saying. I have trouble sometimes." It is important that this opening phrase be sincere and natural, or it can be received as sarcastic and antagonistic. Use the wording that is best suited to your personality and conversational style. In 1651, George Herbert described this idea: "The best mirror is an old friend."

C—Clarify, Correct and Confirm

When the speaker has completed his or her statement or answered a question and you the listener have actively, attentively heard it (step A), have reflected back or mirrored what you heard (step R), the final step is for the speaker to add, subtract, or revise what was said (**clarify** or **correct**) so that both of you agree as to what was meant (**confirm**). The object is not to debate or exchange opinions but only to **understand** each other.

EXERCISE 32

With a friend, coworker, or classmate, practice **attending, reflecting,** and **clarifying-confirming** by taking turns completing these sentences:

1. When in among strangers I feel . . .
2. What I look for and need in a friend . . .
3. What I like most about my job . . .
4. What really irritates me is . . .
5. I really feel satisfied whenever I . . .

When you have finished all five of these exercises, discuss the quality of the reflection. Were you corrected often? If so, you need more practice in being someone's "mirror."

Interview Techniques

You should know, practice, and be proficient in the use of all these interview techniques, so that you can automatically use the right technique at the right time on the right person:

1. **Closed, Direct, or Pointed** questions require either a Yes-no or simple factual reply. They tell you nothing about the person, nor do they provide any additional or background information except for the factual answer. Closed questions are good for confirming the **what** employment history, place-time-date of an event, but poor for determining **how** or **why** or qualitative aspects of what happened. Pointed questions in sensitive areas can be used as a verbal jab to get or keep attention, crash through defenses, or keep the interviews on edge in a stress interview with verbal rifle bullets with crisp word delivery or raised voice and little or no time to think or prepare an answer. A "soft" use of direct questioning is to ask the same question but worded differently several times during the interview to compare and cross-validate answers. Example of simple closed question: "Where were you at 11:00 PM on Monday, November 28, 1988?" Pointed questions: "I know that you don't return home at 11:00 PM every night. Why did you do so then? What was so different about that night? What was on your mind that night at that time?"

2. **Open or Open-Ended** questions work like a fish net, open wide at first, allowing for more than a simple yes or no, then slowly closing as they are answered. The additional information flowing is used as the basis for further questions. This is the type of questioning most recommended by experts. It ensures dialog, 2-way communication, active interaction, and you get more than basic, factual information but also impressions, opinions, and other helpful clues. This technique gives you more time and opportunity to observe nonverbal behaviors and to further evaluate verbal behaviors. Open-ended questions start with **what, what about, how, how about, could it be, would it be correct to say,** or **I wonder what.** Example: "What were you doing Monday night, November 28, 1988?" or "what were your job duties at XYZ Corporation?" It is generally agreed that **why** questions should NOT be used because they invite excuses, opinion (hearsay), and dull the edge of questioning.

3. **Buttering** is beginning a question with a disarming, softening compliment, apology, or appreciation. Examples: "I want to thank you for coming here ... I'm sorry to have to ask you these questions but we

need information on . . . as an experienced _____ I know you're familiar with . . . " You can "butter" **after** an answer: "I can certainly understand that . . . don't blame you . . . I'm not surprised . . . " Even a simple, soft spoken low volume: "Yes" or "uh-huh" helps facilitate information flow and is a form of buttering, a way of saying "thanks for that answer."

4. **Coat-Tailing** is to repeat word-for-word the interviewee's last statement, phrase, or words, as the beginning of your next question. It sounds like you're reflecting, but the technique is used to build your next question according to your strategic plan. The strategy here is that by using the interviewee's own most recent words you "get inside" his or her thoughts and feelings. Example: Interviewee ends with " . . . and I felt the need to leave there right away." Interviewer (slowly): "Felt the need to leave there right away. Why the urgency?"

5. **Columbo Routine.** This is actually a repeated question seeking a second answer and additional information, but done by putting yourself down: "Well, uh, I have trouble understanding sometimes. Like right now. I don't know, I'm a little slow on the uptake, I guess. Uh, would you mind telling me again (or more about) _____?" Use your own words, whatever sounds natural, sincere, and a bit stupid! This can be used to slow down fast talkers and cut down on the "64 dollar words" and jargon of technical or professional interviewees. It can also help detect malingerers, con artists, and psychopaths who **assume** you're not too bright and lower their guard to "move in for the kill" and put you down even more. TV's Columbo is an excellent example of this technique and how it can be an effective verbal bear trap. In 1665, La Rochefoucauld described this technique in his **Maxims:** "There is great ability in knowing how to conceal one's ability."

6. **Mirroring** is the same technique as the reflection step of the ARC method but additional questions are "tacked on" to the end. It is helpful where there isn't enough information and you want to probe answers more deeply. It has been used effectively to slightly change direction, interpretation, or emphasis each time an answer is reflected, to explore other aspects or explanations for an event. It's a subtle "could it be this, that, or the other" line of questioning.

7. **Comparison or Pairing** is to ask how the answer was **like** or **unlike** the previous answer, or to another answer earlier, or to something else. It enables you to broaden the scope of questioning by introducing any other similar fact, situation, or subject. The truth may be somewhere between two similar things or something entirely different. Comparison

questions give you the opportunity to break out of the bounds of the interview up to that point and reach out in other directions, or more deeply into the interviewee's thinking. Example: "You said he was carrying a gun and it scared you. Can you explain that more?" This allows for questions about offender and victim verbal and nonverbal behaviors, such as whether the offender was left or right-handed. The way the gun was carried or used can reflect familiarity with weapons from military, police, or crime syndicate.

8. **Discount** questions contain "put downs" to plant self-doubt in the mind of the interviewee. This technique can be used to test the person's certainty about an answer by giving a verbal shove, or to explore possible motives. The strategy behind this technique is that by pushing a little, the person is put off balance, more apt to respond spontaneously without time to fall back to a safer, more passive defense. Example: "You were in a hurry and your mind was busy with other things, so you probably aren't sure of that." "You really didn't care about what was happening." Some interviewees use discounting as a defense, to minimize guilt and responsibility. Example: The rapist says: "It was 2 AM and she slinked past me, all alone and giving me the come on."

9. **Ole Philosopher** questions seemingly jump off track into the abstract, off the wall, into the big picture. Examples: "But what does it all mean?" Use this technique to dramatically change the conversation, the subject, or the direction of the interview. Can be a test of the interviewee's awareness. Few interviewees will understand the question and fewer still able to answer—but neither is important. The Ole Philosopher (really the ole fox!) technique expands the scope of questioning and enables you to jump ahead farther along, no longer enmeshed in previous questions. If you haven't been getting much valuable or useful information, this enables you to jet off into other conversational worlds.

10. **Humor** is a double-edged sword, dull or sharp, that can cut two ways. Used positively, it is warming, keeps the atmosphere casual and informal, between two fun loving OK Kids. Everybody enjoys a good laugh. Used negatively your heavy-handed, blaming parent cools down the interview and puts down the interviewee's NOT OK Kid. Example: "Wow! I'll bet you never ran faster in your life" (positive). "You didn't break your leg running to the phone to report this crime" (negative). Use humor with care. It can backfire on you or screw up the works and waste valuable time. The safest humor is against yourself, to put yourself down. The best humor is lighthearted, a verbal rubbing or tap, never cutting.

Bill Mauldin, a World War II combat cartoonist, described humor as "really laughing off a hurt, grinning at misery" (*Time,* July 21, 1961).

11. **Silence,** the intentional use of an "electric silence" or "pregnant pause." Used too little and very powerful. Actors and actresses call it "artistic repose." All you need do is stop talking, looking calmly at the interviewee. Many will repeat the last answer with a "let me say it again" or explain it with more details ("Let me make it clearer"). Some interviewers will even **then** sit silently and observe and listen carefully for the interviewee's next move. Silences can bring many important verbal and nonverbal behaviors to the surface, valuable clues to innermost thoughts and feelings, withheld information, guilty knowledge, or forgotten memories. Many are uncomfortable with silences because they can mean approval or disapproval. Some interviewee's impaled on the skewer of silence will ask: "Is something wrong? Shall I answer again? Do you want more?" Use this technique at least once in every interview to check out its possible good effect. Carefully observe nonverbal behaviors during silences for valuable clues to underlying emotions, possibly withheld information or guilty knowledge.

12. **Stress, Pressure, Threat,** can be applied to interviewees by appearing to be uncomfortable, irritated, frustrated, or confused, using nonverbal mannerisms, fumbling with your notes, pen, clothing, or furniture, or verbal behaviors like raising your voice or changing your voice tone, or by increasing the speed of questions. These behaviors increase fear, anxiety, guilt, or anger, depending on the interviewee's attitude, personality, and mental state. If the person is a suspect, this technique can test for "guilty knowledge." If a witness is concealing information, increasing anxiety, fear, or guilt with this technique might bring out that information. Can be applied in repeated verbal prods at opportune times or gradually and continually as Aesop described it 2500 years ago: "Little by little does the trick." Example: "**Why** didn't you **do** something?" "Did it **ever** occur to you, to _____?"

13. **Confusion or Deception.** This is an indirect technique, a deliberate smoke screen to conceal the next or later important question. It can be done with a "loaded" question buried in the conversation or by taking the initiative with wordy comments, opinions, or observations in several directions without waiting for or responding to an answer. They can be statements that actually require no answer or you can ask a series of questions at a time, allowing little or no time for an adequate answer, such as " . . . so is it _____ or _____ or _____ or maybe _____ or

_____?" In many cases, there will be silence. The suspect doesn't know which question to answer first (usually it's the last question). Then, calmly as if you have just vented, you say: "Well, anyway, that's what it seems to me. OK, now about _____?" which is what you **really** want to ask anyway. The strategy here is to apply stress to bring needed information to the surface and out. In his *Maxims,* Napoleon described this tactic: "We often get in quicker by the back door than by the front." A variation of this is to insert the "hot" question among less important questions to observe for any significant verbal or nonverbal response, such as: "Then as you say the baby seemed to be choking. Did you bundle it up tightly with the blanket? What exactly did you do?" "You say she took her clothes off, but did you help her, were any clothes torn?"

14. **Paradox** or exaggeration is creating questions in an opposite or contrasting way, a "devil's advocate" approach. To a seemingly unimportant answer and in a suddenly louder voice you ask: "**You** did **what?**" or "How could you?" Or it can be approving and accepting: "Everybody violates the law at some time or another. Like it says in the Bible "every saint sins seven times a day." Or when the questioned person says: "I guess I'm a real no good son-of-a-bitch," you say: "Yeah, it sure looks like it!" This technique is useful when witnesses try to protect the suspect or in employment interviews when you suspect the applicant is withholding information. It is an outflanking maneuver, doing the unexpected to catch the person off guard. It is an "it takes a thief to catch a thief" tactic in which you **seem** to agree with wrongdoing in order to better get at the truth to stop future wrongdoing. Example: An anonymous person wrote on a school chalkboard: "God is dead, (signed) Freud." Beneath it, in another handwriting: "Freud is dead, (signed) God."

15. **Defuse.** These are "feeling level" comments or questions to calm or slow emotion or to help vent feelings. They "plateau out" emotions which if uncontrolled would interfere with the interview process. These questions do not provide any needed data but vent or stabilize emotion to continue the flow of needed information. Examples: "How do you feel about that?" "What's your opinion of that?" "I know it's uncomfortable for you right now, and I'm sorry about that." Some witnesses tearfully come to a stop. Always have a box of facial tissues within reach. Some are embarrassed to cry and should be told sympathetically: "It's OK to cry. I understand how you feel." While a person who is upset speaks, it's good "active listening" to nod your head and an occasional softly spoken "yes" helps the person continue.

16. **Provocation.** These are quick verbal thrusts done deliberately to provoke a response or to observe interviewee reaction. Examples: In employment interviews: "Why should we hire you?" Crime victim: "Did you say or do anything to cause this crime?" Or at any time in an interview: "Oh? What do you mean by that?" "Why are you fidgeting with your fingers?"

17. **Self-Disclosure.** This is sharing your own thoughts, feelings, previous experiences, attitude, or opinion. Using it help establish and maintain rapport or "fellow feeling," an "equalizer" technique. The real reason it is used, however, is to help facilitate disclosure from the other person. It's an "I'll show you mine if you show me yours" transaction.

18. **Role Play.** This is to reenact the event by taking the part of the victim, witness, or suspect, or asking them to assume the role of another in the reenactment. This technique can uncover new information, evidence, or motives.

While not an interview technique, **slips of the tongue** or **Freudian slips** can occur at any time and are **always** worth further study. They are seemingly only a mispronounced word or a similar word in sound to the one intended. Freud suspected that they often expose deeper thoughts and feelings. Example: The boss, letter in hand, stands before his secretary's messy, cluttered desk and says: "Miss Jones, could you please fix this **litter,** uh, I mean **letter?**" Pretty Patty looks soulfully into Handsome Harry's eyes and coos: "So why don't you **ball me** some time—oh, I mean **call me** some time?" A minister delivers a eulogy of a known womanizer: "He will live in **immorality** —I mean **immortality.**"

EXERCISE 33

Review the interview techniques. Which do you now use routinely? Which do you **not** use at all? Why? Practice **all** of them so that they will be at your finger tips for immediate use. Try videotaping so you can check your verbal and nonverbal delivery. Audiotapes will help you perfect verbal skills.

The Laws of Emotions

Emotions are powerful internal forces difficult to control under stress. Mark Twain described human beings as "the only creature that blushes—

or needs to." In his book *Abinger Harvest*, E. M. Forster observed that "emotions may be endless. The more we express them the more we may have to express." Experienced interviewers and interrogators watch for signs of underlying emotion in voice tone and volume, rate of speech, pauses, word choice, and in nonverbal behaviors such as posture, gestures, mannerisms, and eye contact. They tune in to the feeling level or emotional tone of the interview or interrogation, "go with the flow," and monitor it carefully.

You should be familiar with the **laws of emotion** to better observe and understand those you question. The following is a recent description of how emotions work from a 1988 journal article by Nico Frijda of the University of Amsterdam, Netherlands.

1. **Law of Situational Meaning.** Emotions are reactions to **meaningful events important to the individual.** Examples: Grief from loss; fear when threatened; anger if frustrated; love for an attractive person.

2. **Law of Concern.** Emotions arise in events that relate to **goals, concerns, or motives.** Example: Worry or sorrow for someone in trouble or hurt.

3. **Law of Apparent Reality.** The intensity of emotion is based on what is **perceived as real,** even if it isn't real or if most others do not take it seriously. Example: You are always the first to show up at meetings and social events and you feel fearful and guilty if you arrive on time or late.

4. **Law of Change.** Emotional intensity increases when there is an actual, expected, or imagined **change from the normal.** It is triggered by the changing event, peaks then fades. Examples: Roller coaster ride; exciting sports event; a very funny joke; combat bravado which becomes anxiety and ends in a depressive "let down."

5. **Law of Affective Contrast.** Pleasure or pain seem to decrease by **repetition over time.** Severe stress (pain) is more bearable the longer it continues. Continued pleasure fades in time. As the Pennsylvania Dutch say: "Love don't last; cookin' does." Example: An endless row of hot fudge sundaes would eventually bore you.

6. **Law of Comparative Feeling.** Emotional intensity is influenced by **expectations,** such as chance for success, or an event compared to some other related factor. Example: an empty chair at the dinner table of a deceased loved one who is not **emotionally** considered dead even though everyone consciously knows it to be so.

7. **Law of Asymmetry.** Pleasure depends on change (new sources).

Negative emotions continue as long as negative conditions continue. Examples: You like to eat at a different restaurant to celebrate special occasions because the food tastes better and the setting is "special" each time.

8. **Law of Conservation of Momentum.** Intense emotions from severe stress remain long after the stressful event has ended. Example: Combat veterans, accident and crime victims, survivors of natural catastrophes.

9. **Law of Closure.** Strong emotions seem total and absolute to the person experiencing them. Examples: Total (suicidal) despair; blind (homicidal) rage; overwhelming grief (suicide attempts to join the loved one); being (madly) in love.

10. **Law of Consequences.** Every emotion triggers an opposite or different emotion influenced by possible consequences. The effect is to moderate or attenuate the original emotion. Example: Anger at a crime suspect ("I wanna kill him") controlled because you know you must interrogate him. A depressed loner joins a cult and feels loved and "special."

11. **Law of Lightest Load and Greatest Gain.** If an emotion can be seen in several ways, it will be seen in the most positive, least negative, light. Example: Casual attitude of some child molesters, rapists, and cult members toward their offenses.

EXERCISE 34

Review the eleven laws of emotion. Think of examples you have experienced or have seen. How many of these laws do you see in your everyday life? Use them to better understand the emotional "workings" of those you question.

WHAT YOU SHOULD HAVE LEARNED

You should now know the difference between **interview** and **interrogation**, how to plan for and conduct an interview, your basic communications style (X, Y, or Z), do's and don'ts for effective interviewing, special interview settings (crime victims and witnesses, news gathering, military and industrial intelligence, job interviews, performance evaluation, and stress interviews. You should know and have practiced the **interview techniques** and understood and observed the eleven **laws of emotion**. If you do not have a working knowledge of this material, please go back and review it. You will need this background in order to better understand the interrogation process, the subject of the next and final chapter. If you want to read more about interview interaction, here are recommended additional readings:

Leeds, D. (1987). *Smart questions.* New York: McGraw-Hill.
Nirenberg, J. S. (1973). *Getting through to people.* Englewood Cliffs, NJ: Prentice-Hall.

CHAPTER 5

INTERROGATION

> Interrogation is an art acquired by study,
> practice, and alertness coupled with some
> degree of natural talent . . . noone can teach
> cleverness but any mentally awake person
> can, with proper diligence, become skilled.
>
> Harold Mulbar
> (*Interrogation,* 1951)

Interrogation probes deeper than the interview and seeks information to reach a conclusion of more serious consequence such as confession of a crime, sensitive military or industrial information, or information of national or international significance such as the Watergate break-in. Interrogation **recreates and details an event** or it **obtains indepth information** on a specific subject. Every step of interrogation is like a photo being developed, part of an incident frozen in time. Every question is like the clicking shutter of a **professional** photographer's camera. When errors, misperception, and dead ends are separated out, the assembled information functions like time-lapse photos, a slow motion replay of the event, or chapters in a book, an in-depth study of a specific subject. Done well, the event or the subject is clearly recognizable to witnesses or experts, a near perfect "fit" to reality.

Accurate information leading to a firm conclusion, the object of interrogation, comes from the quality of the questioning and the skill of the interrogator. It requires the reflexes of a boxer, the skill of a surgeon, the precision of a scientist, and the curiosity of a researcher. There are a variety of settings: civil or criminal cases, military or industrial security, investigative reporting or government intelligence. Harold Mulbar commented in his 1951 book, *Interrogation,* that "the weakest link in the collection of evidence is in interrogation," and "cases remain unsolved because some improperly trained official was perfunctory during the interrogation phase." On the other hand, he estimated 99 percent of criminal cases are solved, and by "properly conducted interrogation than by any other means."

Scientific Interrogation

"Properly conducted interrogation" is **scientific**, which means it is carefully planned and highly structured, with intentionally controlled conditions—scientists call that "standard laboratory conditions." This requires that everything in the interrogation process be "standardized," under strict control, close observation, and appropriate documentation, **except for one:** the verbal and nonverbal responses of the person being interrogated. Everything else is not only known, but is an integral part of the interrogation process.

The Scientific Method and Interrogation

To be truly **scientific**, interrogation must follow the 5-step scientific method described in Chapter 1: 1. State the problem; 2. Observe objectively; 3. Gather data; 4. Evaluate; 5. Conclude. Scientific interrogation is based on these five steps and other factors unique to the interrogation setting described in this chapter. Here is the 5-step scientific interrogation method:

1. SET THE STAGE (same as **state the problem, goal, terms**)
   This is the planning stage and requires these steps:

   Know the case, all available information (what's there)
   Know what information you need (what isn't there)
   Prepare the room (standard laboratory conditions)
   Prepare yourself (style, approach, adapted to needs)

2. INTERACTION (same as **observation**)
   This is the "meat" of the interrogation sandwich:

   Warmup and introductions, from the instant of meeting the suspect to sitting, sharing. You stand for a moment as suspect sits, file folder in your hand, a strong, subliminal nonverbal message. Verbal: "Mr. Jones, I'm Detective Mary Smith and I'm here to talk to you about the rape in Adams Park on Tuesday night, November 29th."
   Objective observation, throughout the interrogation.
   Nonverbal: All factors describe in Chapter 3 and elsewhere, especially mannerisms when meeting such as quality of handshake, eye contact.
   Verbal: All factors described in Chapter 3 and 4 and in this chapter.

Confrontation, hard or soft, after Re-Mirandizing. A judgment call based on the case and the suspect.

Hard: "Mr. Jones, the evidence here points to you as the offender." Always use a full file folder even if it's full of blank paper. Do *not* say: "Mr. Jones, you did it."

Soft: "Mr. Jones, we need more information to close this case and I appreciate your willingness to talk with me about it."

Working through. The give-and-take "work" of interaction between you and the suspect, selecting questions and techniques, communications skills, managing problems.

3. GATHER DATA

   This is the original database of statements, reports, and evidence, new information from the interrogation, and your interpretations of verbal and nonverbal behaviors.

4. EVALUATE

   This occurs during as well as after interrogation and is an ongoing assessment of the database as to quality and quantity, and what is needed to further refine it, consolidate what's there and sharpen the focus for the final conclusion, the confession.

5. CONCLUSION

   The confession or final, conclusive report in investigative reporting, military or industrial intelligence.

Interrogation Standards

In addition to these five **steps** of the scientific method, there are minimal **standards** for effective **scientific** interrogation:

Physical Setting. Just as in interviewing, physical surroundings for effective interrogation should be conducive to obtaining needed information. Experienced interrogators agree that most offenders want to confess and have a psychological and emotional need to do so. The room in which interrogation takes place should facilitate this need. It should be **quiet, comfortable,** and **private.** Interruptions can be disastrous and **must be prevented.** They give offenders time to review what has been said and choose better defenses to evade questioning. They interrupt your train of thought. You may not return to the same question, may skip ahead and fail to get important data. You may not return to questioning with exactly the same edge or focus. They stop the conversation, slow the pace and momentum that took time to develop. To protect against these negative effects there should be no phone in the interrogation room. A prominent DO NOT DISTURB sign should be placed outside the door with ROOM VACANT on the other side. Everyone will then know exactly when the room is in use, keep the outside noise level down, and quickly assist if the person interrogated becomes violent—rare but possible, and in **scientific** interrogation all possibilities are considered.

Taping. Interrogation should be taped, preferably videotaped. VHS equipment is now inexpensive and with automatic focus and long-play tape. This allows you to use the tape consulting with arresting officers, other experienced interrogators, or expert consultants, and later with release of information, training purposes. It is **live** and **real life** material you can use to improve your own strategy and tactics in the future. Videotaping can also be done through a 1-way mirror to minimize distraction. If you use only audiotaping, use smaller recorders. They are visually less obvious. A huge recorder with large microphone in front of you and the cassette wheels rotating is NOT conducive to free and open conversation. Some interrogation rooms have a small "bug" mike and the recorder in an adjacent room. If you use this method, be certain there's an operator to switch to fresh tapes. There's nothing like making a big breakthrough only to discover the tape ran out and you have nothing but your memory to rely on!

Furniture and Furnishings. More attention should be given to furniture placement and furnishings for interrogation than for interview. The best room should not be larger than ten by twelve feet, with a small desk against a wall (**never** between you and the suspect), and at least two comfortable chairs facing each other. The suspect should be in full view at all times so that you can closely observe both verbal and nonverbal behaviors, just like a scientific experiment. No smoking should be allowed, a subtle way of applying some stress. There should be a NO SMOKING sign prominently mounted on the wall and no ashtrays, lighters, or matches. If you are a smoker, leave your tobacco outside so you can quickly dispense with any "got a smoke?" requests by saying simply you don't smoke. There should be no "sharps" or "throwables" in the room and windows and framed pictures should have shatterless glass or plastic. Some suspects have gone through windows in an effort to escape, unknowingly from an upper floor. Suspects should not be handcuffed. You should not be in uniform nor have your weapon with or on you. You should not block the doorway by sitting between the door and the suspect. You increase risk of injury by blocking the door and backup outside the room will prevent escape.

Setting the Stage. You should sit in front of or slightly to the side of the suspect, close enough so that your knees almost (but don't) touch. As questioning continues and you move "closer to the truth" you can gradually "move in" by first leaning forward, then if you choose, moving your chair closer. With males, you can in time move your knee between his, but females may react defensively or "freeze up" and withdraw psychologically from the close questioning needed. Any male-female interrogator-suspect should be witnessed or the door left slightly ajar. This is not as critical if you are videotaping. Think of the room as a laboratory and interrogation as a carefully controlled experiment. Like a research scientist, you proceed to recreate an event, detail by detail, with only one variable: the suspect. The whole process is focussed on it, moving from the unknown to the known. That process begins in the room itself, before any words are exchanged.

EXERCISE 35

Alone or if possible, with others who will be interrogating, make a survey of the room used. Check the lighting, type of furniture and its placement, decor and wall color, curtains and carpeting, acoustics, recording equipment (age, quality of recording). Should the room be improved? If so, how?

The Criminal Mind

The diagnostic manuals of psychiatry (the DSMs) do not list assault, murder, rape, arson, robbery, or child abuse as signs of mental illness. They are **crimes**, and those who commit them are **criminals**, yet most are **legally sane** or are committed to receive treatment until **legally competent** to stand trial. A licensed mental health professional must certify that he understands the charges, courtroom procedure, and the legal process, and can assist in their defense. What criminals do when they violate the law and hurt people is most certainly not "normal." They suggest a deranged, depraved, or **abnormal** mind.

The Nazi Mind? Personality testing was done on eight leading Nazi war criminals at Spandau prison after World War II. In those days, the world was so shocked at their brutality that they referred to "the Nazi mind." This made it easier to separate good (us) from evil (them). We didn't have to look within ourselves for such violent tendencies. Some early, relatively superficial test interpretations agreed with this over-simplification, but in 1946 Kelley concluded that Nazi personalities are "not unique or insane" and "could be duplicated in any country of the world today" (p. 47). In 1978 Ritzler reviewed the test material, agreed the tested Nazi leaders were not psychotic, and suggested they may have been opportunistic "successful psychopaths." In 1989, Zillmer, Archer, and Castino reviewed these and other studies and reevaluated the test data using the latest scoring system and two separate computer programs. They found a variety of personality problems in seven of the eight Nazis, possible thought disorder in four, but poor impulse control in only two. These researchers concluded there was a wide variety of personality dynamics and while they deviated somewhat from normal behavior they had little in common: "Although Nuremberg revealed to the world the terrible crimes committed by Hitler's followers, the use of any overall descriptors to attempt to summarize the personality functioning of this group appears unjustified" (p. 98). In short, there is no such thing as "the Nazi mind." Stated another way, the kind of persons who became Nazis are with us today in every city and nation.

Force of Evil? There are references to evil as a force throughout history, in every society, every culture. In the *Old Testament*, the first evil described is temptation, when Adam and Eve ate the forbidden fruit. Lucifer, **the** devil, was first an angel, then a "fallen" angel. Cain and Abel were brothers, one good, the other evil. So, thousands of years ago, the Hebrews described how evil is within us. The New Testament describes how Judas was selected by Jesus, one of the first disciples. He managed the money, a trusted position, yet betrayed his leader and is today the symbol of deceit. There are similar themes in drama and music. Shakespeare's *MacBeth* and also *Hamlet* describe ruthless ambi-tion that stops at nothing, not even murder. Robert Louis Stevenson, a physician, wrote *Dr. Jekyll and Mr. Hyde*, a classic tale of evil within a person and also an example of **multiple personality disorder**. *Faust* was a 16th century doctor who sold his soul to the devil for youth and power. That legend inspired the music of Berlioz, Gounod, and Liszt and Thomas Mann and Goethe wrote of it. The common thread through all these is that evil is a force, deeply rooted in history worldwide, and it is within us. We are daily surrounded by evidence of it, in every day's newspaper and TV newscasts evil is reported in its many forms—crime, cruelty, illegal and unethical practices, war.

The evil mind? What is there in the mind that impels people to hurt others? Some mental health professionals estimate that as many as one in four adults were physically or sexually abused as children, to the point that it affects their personality and adjustment. Studies prove that many abused children grow up to be abusing parents. Many children of alcoholics and drug abusers follow their parents into substance abuse. The same is true for many spouse abusers. This suggests that in many cases these antisocial behaviors are learned. Some researchers have reported abnormal brain waves and biochemical imbalance in the brains of some convicted criminals. Are they "wired wrong?" Is it somehow tied in to body chemistry? Or as more experts are beginning to report, is it a combination of factors, our old friends heredity (brain and body) *and* environment (learning and conditioning)? In law there is *malum in se*, inherently wrong, and *malum prohibitum* crimes, wrong because society (law) defines it as wrong.

EXERCISE 36

Share in class or with a coworker the phenomenon of evil. What is evil? Who has it? How does evil differ by degree (murder vs shoplifting) and by person (child and adult, first time offender, habitual minor crimes, syndicate crime)? How can your opinion and belief help or hinder you as an interrogator?

Your MOM—and Crime!

MOM stands for **motive, opportunity,** and **means.** These are the three elements which when present increase the likelihood a crime will be committed. **Motive** is the inner, deeper motivation or urge, a "mental motor" running inside, that drives the criminal on. Motive to commit crime can be for money needed to buy drugs, the "high" or peak excitement experienced by serial killers, sadists, and psychopaths, a burning rage against women of a Jack the Ripper, or the predatory instinct or misdirected sex drive toward a child or mentally ill or retarded victim. **Opportunity** is the cue or stimulus, the chance or carefully planned situation, in which the motive is unleashed. **Means** is the weapon, trap, or trick, to satisfy a motive at the opportune time to commit the crime.

Most criminals are impulsive. They have very weak ego and emotional controls. They have great difficulty managing their emotions and "delaying gratification"—they seek to satisfy their needs quickly and directly, regardless of consequences. Those who molest children or take sexual advantage of a vulnerable adult are channeling an otherwise healthy sex drive into a socially and psychologically harmful and unlawful act. Most offenders **do** have emotions and have some awareness that what they have done is unlawful and has injured the victim, physically or mentally. Effective interrogators can tap these selfish emotions and use them to get a confession. There are other criminal types who are emotionally cool, described by many as "without conscience." They are **sociopaths** or **psychopaths,** difficult to interrogate because of being emotionally and socially aloof, outside morals and standards, and more difficult if they are also of above average intelligence.

Sociopaths and Psychopaths

Sociopaths and **psychopaths** are two deep-seated, usually lifelong, personality patterns that involve antisocial behavior. Some experts believe they are formed by age 6 (Glueck and Glueck, 1950). Neither are listed in the DSM diagnostic manual as mental disorders, even though they are considered by some authorities to be a type of psychosis (Cleckley, 1941). Others suggest they are caused by a combination of emotional deprivation and child abuse (Guttmacher, 1953). Some suggest it may be an **organic** condition, a form of brain damage, since parts of the brain and midbrain are involved in pleasure, and hostile anger. Lab rats will die of starvation repeatedly tapping electrodes to their brain's pleasure center. Perhaps a homicidal rage, killing and killing, does the same. Currently, **antisocial personality disorder** is the only mental disorder listed in the DSM which most closely relates to sociopaths and psychopaths but DSM criteria omits much of the qualities described here. They can and often do have features of other personality disorders (borderline, narcissistic, avoidant, paranoid, passive-aggressive, and obsessive-compulsive). They differ from all these by their recognizable, repeated pattern of behavior and distinctive lifestyle beyond social values and the law, of crime or violence.

Sociopaths disregard or violate social or legal standards. Examples are derelicts, drunk drivers, habitual gamblers, prostitutes, and the alcohol or drug dependent. Usually they are "losers" and "loners" who live and work in the shadows, "out of it" and "not with it" by societal standards. They are self-destructive in an indirect, passive way, by the cost in money, time, energy, dignity, pain or discomfort to themselves and others. **Spongers** are sociopaths who "milk" what they want from **suckers**, well meaning, naive helpers and rescuers. Those who don't "give" are known by sociopaths as **bastards.**

Psychopaths also disregard social and legal standards but do so more directly, such as in crime or ruthless "cut throat" business or political practices. Some are very intelligent and seem to get a special high outwitting the police and victims (Ex. certain serial killers). Crime and violence are especially exciting to them, even funny in a gruesome, grotesque way. They seem especially excited having an innocent victim under their complete control, to do with as they choose, life and death power. The senseless cruelty and viciousness of some of their crimes is an evidence of this. Other psychopathic personalities are less direct. They build personal power through clever self-promotion and strong hypnotic-like charisma. Even religion is not immune from them, sinners who masquerade as saints (Example: Jimmy Jones of Jonestown where 913 of his followers killed themselves). It is likely that wars have been caused by psychopaths in high office with a support staff of sociopaths (Examples: Hitler, Stalin). A psychopath can build a thriving drug business wholesaling to sociopathic dealers.

Psychopaths can be difficult to interrogate, especially if of above average intelligence. They are like undersocialized savages, untamed animals, and they usually have the eyes of a predator. Go to a zoo and look into the eyes of a gorilla, lion, or tiger. Those eyes look back, at and through you. Somehow, psychopaths have never learned and do not feel the need to conform to normal, sharing behavior or to social responsibility. Their personalities are fixed, rigid, and most have very well developed defenses from years of combat against society. The fact that they are still here, in front of you as for interrogation, proves they are survivors in a war against society. The following checklist of characteristics of the psychopathic personality are paraphrased from Cleckley (1941): superficial charm or intelligence; no delusions or irrational thoughts; little or no anxiety; unreliable; insincere and untruthful; crime hardly justifies motive or payoff; no remorse or shame; poor judgment; selfish, unable to love; lacks feeling, emotionally poor; lacks insight; not really friendly; alcohol or drugs lower self-control; talks suicide, rarely acts on it; superficial sex life; no really meaningful life goals.

They tend to be reckless, selfish, impulsive thrill seekers who get high on violence and getting back at society, at authority figures like you. A frequent motive of rapists is to get even and pay back women, either for being rejected by them or as a punishing mother figure. They are generally insensitive to pain or a need to change or correct their destructive behavior, opportunists and manipulators who have learned or who have a predatory instinct to size up, set up, and use people. They appear to have no conscience or compassion, though some can fake caring feelings quite well to get what they want. They can be convincing liars, to the point of successfully eluding polygraph, sodium amytal, or hypnosis interviews. Beneath their smoke screen of faked feelings they are icy cold, incapable of love, guilt, shame, depression, or anxiety except about getting caught. Loners by nature, they are not capable of establishing or maintaining an ongoing close emotional relationship with anyone. They are, to a great extent, in love with themselves. Because they don't set down roots, with people or places, they are drifters who change jobs often and move frequently. If of above average intelligence, their approach to crime is clever and ingenious, and they are and have been the master criminals throughout history, craftsmen of crime. If you ever want to meet the devil or be in the presence of very near 100 percent pure evil this side of Hell, interrogate an intelligent psychopath!

Minor Crimes

It may seem surprising that first time offenders are sometimes more difficult to interrogate than repeat offenders. Shoplifters are a good example. Almost half are store employees. Many of the others can easily afford the products they steal. Factors that have been cited: reaction to stress; to get help or attention; excitement, a "dare" or "game"; depression; impulse; need. As you can see, petty theft is widespread and the reasons are many and varied. Those apprehended may not see what they have done as serious. That means they do not feel emotionally involved enough to show verbal or nonverbal behaviors of guilt. In doing so, they may in their interrogation behaviors resemble psychopaths.

Interrogation Strategy

The **master plan** or **major strategy** of interrogation is to gather as much data as possible then by careful analysis, by exclusion and exception, remove all other possibilities so that what remains is the truth, reality, the information needed, which leads of and by itself to a firm, irrefutable conclusion. Stated another way, it is breaking down all that is known into smaller bits and pieces and analyzing them in greater detail. Ovid, a poet in ancient Rome, wrote in the 8th century AD: "The mightiest rivers lose their force when split up into several streams." **Attention to detail** is the mortar and incisive questions are the bricks or stones in the fortress of **scientific** interrogation.

It may be a tired old saying to you, but still very true: **plan your work** then **work your plan.** Strategic planning is absolutely essential for effective interrogation. You **must** thoroughly review all available material on the case, the evidence and reports, victim, witnesses and suspect, and every possible motive. With this database, you then carefully formulate the best questions to get the needed information which, added to what you already have, leads to a firm conclusion. **Scientific** interrogation is like developing a photograph of the event, or like a slow motion or stop action videotape of it, chronologically and in the greatest detail possible. A skilled interrogator makes it all look easy. As Mark Twain said: "It usually takes me three weeks to prepare a good impromptu speech." There are certain priorities to recognize in strategic planning:

Time and **Patience.** It takes time to plan then do interrogation. Quite often, planning and ongoing analysis can take longer than actual questioning. None of these important functions should be rushed. There's a Zen saying that "when the apple is ripe it drops from the tree of its own weight." Confessions naturally flow from an orderly, logical, paced movement from the unknown to the known, building in force 'til the "big apple" falls. This requires patience on your part. The British statesman Edmund Burke wrote in 1790 that "patience will achieve more than force." Time is on your side. Use it well.

Choose Questions and Techniques Carefully, as a skilled craftsman chooses just the right tool or an artist chooses brush and color. Part of this skill is knowing **what** to ask at just the **right time,** in just the **right way.** Start with the most obvious and most established facts such as the crime or event itself, date, time, general area and specific location, selected evidence, and possible motives. Imagining yourself as the offender can help you explore motives and form questions about them. **Only then** should questions be worded, listed, reviewed and revised to sharpen (or deliberately blur) focus, then arranged in a final sequence, strung like beads in a necklace or links in a strong chain.

Most interrogators start with **open** (open-ended) questions and use **closed** (pointed) questions when there is enough information to sharpen their focus. You should, however, be **flexible,** able to switch back and forth on the inevitable and unpredictable verbal side trips yet return fully on course, like piloting a boat or plane against adverse wind and current. In his 1938 play, *Galileo,* the German playwright Bertold Brecht wrote: "If there are obstacles, the shortest line between two points may be the crooked line."

Self Control. Remaining cool under fire, under stress, is a needed positive trait for interrogators. Learn to insulate yourself emotionally from any revulsion or disgust. If you react during interrogation it can cloud your judgment and interfere with efficiency. Worse still, your anger or impatience might cause you to "strong arm" or coerce a confession from an innocent person. That should **never** happen. Vent your feelings after the session preferably with the help of a coworker, so you don't take it home. The common sense philosopher Josh Billings gave this good advice: "The best time to hold your tongue is the time you feel like you must say something or bust." Napoleon, no stranger to anger and frustration, considered the strong to be those who "can intercept at will the communication between the senses and the mind." Think about it. Develop your self-control.

Maintain Self-Confidence. By now, in your reading of this book and doing the exercises up to this page, together with your life experience as a human being and your training, you should feel more competent—and you are! It means you will be better able now to plan an effective strategy, study the case or subject, victims, witnesses, and suspects, questions to be asked and when and how to ask them, and the best techniques to achieve your goals. Isn't that impressive? If you're ever in a rut and feeling down, refer back to this page and to the list above. Also, refocus yourself, renew your interest and your belief in what you're doing, that it does have value and meaning. You **do** make a difference! Protect your self-confidence.

Doom's Day Machine. There are days when nothing goes well. It's like that flip side of Rudyard Kipling's inspirational poem *If:* "If you can keep your head when all those about you are losing theirs" **you don't really understand the situation!** There are other sayings: It's hard to keep calm when you're up to your ass in alligators! Or the bumper sticker: **Shit happens.** Despite your self confidence and skill, there will be times when everything seems to go wrong. It is then you need your own secret weapon, your own **doom's day machine** to keep you going, a mental magic carpet to carry you far above the dismal village of Toiletsville.

Realize and reflect on that fact that you have a job to do, a responsibility, a duty to perform, not unlike soldiers in combat, surgeon to patient, entertainers who believe "the show must go on," airline pilots at the controls of a crashing plane to the very second of impact. These people know it's better to be doing something useful to the end, even when you **feel** useless. For you, it means concentrating on what you are doing and need to do and to keep doing it. Do as Alcoholics Anonymous teaches, take it one step at a time. Easy does it. Follow your plan. Don't stop. Ask the questions, one by one. Build the information, page by page. Anxiety, worry, depression are all forms of mental **energy.** Use that energy to **push you up** and not just to **pull you down,** to move **in** to the work and not **out** of it or **from** it. Like the martial arts, learn to use the enemy's force to **your** advantage.

Other tips: center yourself in your Adult. Let your OK Kid out to play. Do something childish (eat a double dip ice cream cone). Limber up and laugh a little. Don't take yourself so seriously. Relax more. Take a long, slow deep breath and picture a quiet, restful place. Be there in your mind just for a moment. This is a form of meditation. Keep your muscles loose and limber. When you're tense, so are your muscles. You can't be tense if your muscles are loose. Do one or more of these relaxation techniques every day. If this is difficult for you, "fake it 'til you make it." In *Hamlet,* Shakespeare wrote: "Assume a virtue if you have it not" and in time, with practice, it becomes real for you. Life is a choice. You can choose **not** to be rattled or down. Henry Ford said: "Whether you think you can make it or can't—you're right!" You **are** what you think. Mark this page and use it as an "anti-stress shot."

EXERCISE 37

Watch local TV news interviewers on news, nationwide "talk shows" (*Oprah Winfrey, Donahue, Geraldo*), and Sunday weekly news interviews (*David Brinkley, Meet the Press, Face the Nation, Evans-Novak, MacNeil-Lehrer*). "Track" their line of questioning, their strategy. Observe the verbal and nonverbal behaviors when giving questions and answers. Would you question differently? How is your verbal and nonverbal behavior similar? Different? How can yours be improved?

Tactics and Techniques

In his 1949 autobiography, Will Rogers wrote that "plans get you into things but you got to work your way out." All the recommendations for interviewing described in the previous chapter also apply to interrogation, and they, together with the following tactics and techniques, will get you **through** and **out** of your plan.

1. **Personal Appearance.** Yes, this **is** an interrogation technique and an important one, because your appearance makes you approachable or distancing to the subject, before any words are spoken. You are half of every interrogation interaction. You should **look** receptive not opinionated, open to conversation, yet like you know what you're doing, like someone who **knows** —about the crime or subject, the suspect, evidence, the law, but who also knows and likes people and is interested in talking with the subject on a personal level as equals. Dress the part, not too formal, not sloppy, well groomed. Dress tastefully, without flashy clothes or jewelry, strong aftershave or perfume, gum chewing, candies or breath mints, and sit comfortably upright, hands relaxed in your lap or on your thighs.

2. **Miranda "Rights."** Before any interrogation can begin, you must have the person's **informed consent** to be questioned if not charged with a crime, or inform them of their rights if they have been charged with a crime. This is required by law, from the **Miranda vs Arizona** (1966) U. S. Supreme Court ruling that charged suspects must be "warned" they have a right to remain silent, need not answer questions but if they do, answers can be used in evidence against them, they have a right to legal counsel before or during questioning and if they can't afford one, an attorney will be appointed to represent them without cost to them. They also have the right to stop your interrogation at any time and you are legally bound to comply at once. These statements must be given in clear language and understood by the suspect who then can waive or invoke these rights at any time. If waived, they can answer any and all questions or spontaneously confess to the charges. Miranda rights do not apply to anyone being questioned who has not been charged. Interrogation should not take place until charges are of legal record after a preliminary hearing or arraignment in a federal court. It should be standard practice to "Mirandize" charged suspects before interrogation *and* before a confession is signed.

3. **Rapport.** Looking and behaving like a "pro" does NOT mean to be

"holier than thou," with a snobbish air of superiority. This is **not** the same as nor the sign of competence. You **must** be accepted by the suspect to open and continue free flow of information. To achieve this you must adapt to the suspect's language and meaning. Painful as it may be, you must meet on the same level. If you do not, you cannot really understand him or her. You will not be able to weigh, compare, or see through what is said, and choose the best question to put at the best time. "Flying blind" despite what the suspect says, does, thinks, or feels can result in a cat and mouse game or battle of wits, a waste of time and energy. Good rapport does **not** mean "being a Patsy" or a "mutual admiration society." The secret of **effective** rapport is to show **concern** for the suspect and the seriousness of the charge. This begins the instant you introduce yourself or enter the interrogation room and re-Mirandizing.

Signs of Good Rapport: suspect sits comfortably, leaning forward as if "to meet you half way," uses first names, matches **your** relaxed tone of voice to verbally "meet you half way." **Signs of poor rapport:** suspect "distances" you verbally by using a title (officer, sergeant, mister, miss, ms, doctor, reverend, judge), answering evasively or coldly, or nonverbally by withdrawing, sitting back in the chair, avoiding eye contact, or escaping into physical mannerisms. **Signs of opposition:** arms folded tightly, hand to mouth, hands clasped in front of mouth or on lap, clenched fist, legs crossed, standing up, or pacing the room. These negative effects serve a useful purpose: they tell you the suspect is more closed than open. Carefully choose the best countermeasure: **confront it** by referring to the behavior specifically, with reassurance; **deescalate** by not referring to it but lower your voice and slow your rate of speech (nonverbal reassurance); **take no action,** ignore it and keep going as before; **escalate,** accelerate your delivery and raise your voice (bring it to a head).

4. **Empathize and Agree.** Of all interrogation techniques, this one is the most useful and has been proven far superior to previous more confrontive, judgmental methods. **Empathy** is "fellow feeling," to "put yourself in another's shoes," that "but for the grace of God go I" feeling. It is **not** sympathy, which is feeling sorry for someone. You will be dealing with people who have done things so shocking you could never sympathize with them. But you **must** understand them or you will never be able to plan and use effective questions. To use this technique, first **study** all the background information on the case or the subject as an individual, reflecting all these against the background of your education,

training, and experience in your career and as a human being. You then **adapt** to the person interrogated to such a degree you "get inside" as a good actor or actress does, to know how he or she thinks and feels. Under the same circumstances what would **you** have done, even if to a lesser degree? No one is 100 percent good or 100 percent evil. That includes you. Even the Bible says, "I do not do the good I want, but the evil I do not want is what I do" (Romans 7,19). So, find the "good" in the person interrogated and build rapport on it. Will Rogers, the great humorist and common sense philosopher, said that he never met anyone he didn't like. Hitler was kind to his dog. The famous bank robber Willie Sutton commented, "It's a rather pleasant experience to be alone in a bank at night."

Here are some ways of using the empathy and agree technique: Criticize the victim, the suspect's parents, bosses, others, or life itself. Big corporations can stand to lose some materials, so "taking" isn't really "stealing." Women who dress and walk that way at 1 AM are "looking for it." Criticize society and its double standard of punishment for "personal" crimes and reward for "corporate" or large scale crime, such as Eugene O'Neill's description in his play *Emperor Jones:* "The little stealin' gits you in jail . . . for the big stealin' they makes you emperor and puts you in the Hall of Fame when you croaks." Externalize and minimize blame. In this way, the subject feels you accept him or her as a person. Mention as many minimizing factors as possible. Pick the least revolting, most acceptable reason for the crime and offer it as the major motive. This "friendly fellow feeling" approach makes a big difference, in many cases *the* difference in successful interrogation, as many confessed criminals have said in postconfession interviews.

With reassuring words, tone of voice, and mannerisms (pat on the knee, touch on the arm, handshake), patient and attentive listening, questions reflecting genuine interest as a friend would inquire what happened, move toward confession, such as: "The best thing to do is to settle the matter, close the book, close the door, confess and be done with it. If you were my best friend, my own brother, that's exactly what I'd tell you." As the suspect warms to the idea, pour on more fuel, with something like "and it's the **right** thing to do, the **honorable** thing, the **best for all concerned.**" Ask: "Who do you respect (or love) most in the whole world?" Then refer to that person: "If your grandmother was sitting here instead of me, that's what she would say to you, too, I'm sure of it." It's a selling job, pure and simple. If you have difficulty using this technique, think of yourself as an Academy Award actor or actress. Quite often you have to do things when you're not in the mood for it. This is no different. Remember, you can vent feelings afterward with a coworker and take a shower when you get home. This **is** a **powerful** technique and you should work hard to use it and to perfect it.

5. **Sweet Talk** or **Buttering** is part of the empathy-agree technique. Once you have a trusting relationship with the suspect, there will be open, free conversational flow. You will know it by verbal and nonverbal signs: the equal flow of conversation and its more personal content, and by the relaxed posture and mannerisms of the subject. A skilled interrogator is like the diplomat described in Caskie Stinnett's 1960 book *Out of the Red* who "can tell you to go to hell in such a way you actually look forward to the trip."

6. **Sandwiching** or **Stinger**, also known as **bait** or **bait and switch**. This technique enables you to pair a positive with a negative statement, a verbal "one-two punch." The question begins with a **reassuring positive** followed by **the stinger**: "Now, John, I'm not saying you could ever do such a thing (or think this way) but could it be that _____?" Or: "I apologize for even asking you, but has anything like this ever happened to you before?" (knowing it did and you have the record). Another (Columbo sandwich): "John, maybe you can help me with this. From our talk here I can tell you understand a lot about human nature and I respect your opinion. Who do you think did this? What would motivate a person to?" Toward the end of a session, as a quick reflex test: "Good. Good, John, you've really been helpful and I thank you for the information. Yes. I'll be talking to others and it may be useful to ask everyone to have another session using hypnosis, sodium amytal, or the polygraph. Would that be OK for you?" Or substitute a **Columbo** for the lie tests ending: "I believe you, John. But when I write all this, I want to be sure I make it very clear why you couldn't have done it. I want to be sure it's right. I'd appreciate your help with it. Could you sum that up for me?"

Other Examples. To an incest suspect: "Your daughter, Eva, is certainly a beautiful child and as her father it's obvious to me you love her very much. But love has many forms. Most of us learn about sex on the street, not the best way, so I could see how someone might _____." If you are a parent, you can add an extra slice of ham to the verbal sandwich about also being a parent, proud of your kids. What the hell, show him a photo! For a **sandwich** to become a **stinger** it ends with a bite, a bang, something like "and what about you, John? Is that what you did?" Some

sweet talk can be sprinkled beforehand: "I don't blame you, John. I could see how maybe I would do it, too." Expert interrogators weave techniques together for best focus and effect, like strands in a strong rope.

7. **Dutch Uncle** is the "tough love" approach, talking hard common sense. This technique is used on the rare occasions when "sweet talk" doesn't work. It can be done **gradually** or **suddenly**. To do it gradually is a smooth transition from an "I'm only trying to help you" approach, through **mild disapproval** ("Can't you see that?") to a "Dutch Uncle" hard line confrontation. The change from soft to hard with comments that are still supportive, such as: "It's like I said before, if you were my own brother I'd tell you the same thing" but in a voice with more impatience and frustration. This is reinforced by referring back to some previous admissions, commenting "and you admitted that yourself." Throw in some hard facts from evidence at the scene or known facts that implicate the suspect, with "and what do you think the court's gonna do with all that and everything else that comes out? If you were the judge or jury what would **you** think?" If the suspect says: "I'd think I was innocent" give him or her the horse laugh with: "You gotta be kidding." Add: "And this is gonna go on and on, forever, because the law never gives up. I get tired and you get tired but like *Ole Man River,* the law's always there on the books." To use this technique **suddenly** just stop talking, or draw back and sit up straight, or throw both hands up with: "Oh my God! I don't believe this!" or "Are you for real? Don't you have any idea what you're saying. I can't believe it." If you have a talent for acting and can work up a flushed face with impressive gestures, this one can be quite effective. This technique was reported as early as 100 BC by the slave poet Publilius Syrus: "A tough wedge for a tough log."

8. **Lying, Contradictions, Inconsistencies.** Suspects in criminal cases or anyone who knows of wrongdoing that could cost them their job or reputation have a motive to lie. In his 1987 book *The Art of Questioning,* the noted attorney Peter Megargee Brown pointed out that "catching liars is an art anyone can learn." They show "telltale signs . . . body language provides a rich source of information because certain facial and muscle movements cannot be faked" (p. 25). There are many forms of lying, with up or down moods (anger, defensiveness, or depression), fright (nervous mannerisms, suspiciousness), fight (blaming, irritable), or flight reactions (evasive, unconcerned). Liars can hide behind a smoke screen of anger, shocked innocence, pride and threats to sue, or excessive religiosity. They can be overly cooperative and agreeable, or nitpick on

finer points of information or evidence, usually to explain away, minimize or soften the crime (like blaming the victim). They are often deceptive, giving wrong, misleading, tangential or incomplete answers. Not surprisingly, they tend to overuse defense mechanisms and pause in answering to keep you away from them and the truth. Truthful people can show some of these behaviors but experienced interrogators can observe which deviate from normal and suggest guilty knowledge. Truthful people show more concern emotionally, consistently and sustained, than those who lie, whose emotional intensity usually fades over time. As Thomas Mann wrote in *Magic Mountain:* "Time cools, time clarifies. No mood can be maintained quite unaltered through the course of hours."

Confronted with what you know to be a lie, you can move in or wait them out, let them lie more and more, hopefully in greater detail, and note each false statement. From time to time, you can weave in what you can prove to be an "error" when asking a question later, with a comment something like "just before, you mentioned that _____. Now that can't be, because _____. Could you be mistaken?" This tells the suspect you caught him in a lie, gives him a chance to "save face" and gives you another shot at getting the facts you wanted the first time. If the lies or contradictions continue, select two or three and softly confront again saying something like "well now, there are several things that just don't add up, like _____. I want to go over them again, one at a time, because you're memory of them isn't correct. I want to be sure I get them right because they may come up in court and could be considered perjury. That would mean even more charges against you. I'm sure you wouldn't want that." Note that strong words like **lie, truth,** and **wrong** are omitted. If later answers are suspected to be lies, use silence, sit calmly, do nothing, looking (don't stare) at the suspect, and wait him or her out. Such silences "heat up the stove" and make it uncomfortable. The suspect may correct the answer before you have to say anything. Generally, this technique overcomes defenses better than a verbal frontal assault like: "You're lying, wasting my time and yours." Verbal honey **does** work better than vinegar. On the other hand, you can overcome lying and inconsistencies by shifting from a soft (sympathy-agree) to a harder (Dutch Uncle) approach without "verbal combat."

9. **Lying and deception—Yours!** Should **you** lie? Interesting question. If you can get the needed information without deception, do so. "Trickery" and "deceit" on your part can cause problems by the defense attorney in

court, though some deception has been allowed in many state and federal cases. A handy rule is the effect the deception would have on the innocent: it should not lead an innocent person to make a false confession nor "shock the conscience." As a general rule, do not lie — but have a flexible imagination! In certain specific cases, where you have made a cost-benefit analysis of the importance of the information vs. the possible damage to the case in court, deception is acceptable. Examples: "If someone said they saw you going into the bar late that night, would they be correct?" Or: "Your friend, John, has told us a lot about you that day." "We have a lot of fingerprints from the room we're analyzing right now." If none of these statements is true, technically you're lying and being deceptive. Consult with legal counsel to be certain you don't jeopardize your case.

10. **Wide Net.** In the islands of the South Seas, men stand waist deep in the sea and throw a weighted hand net that strikes the water's surface in a near perfect circle. It drops beneath the waves to capture more fish than a net poorly thrown that would hit the water more closed. Interrogation should begin with an expertly thrown wide net. It will catch more fish! "Did you kill Jane Doe?" is a narrow net with a 50-50 chance of a "No!" answer that alerts the "fish" to the trap and preps it for the same negative, defensive, resistance to further questioning. Repeated, this negative pattern hardens, becomes even more entrenched. The technique described above to cope with lying is a **wide net** tactic, moving from facts which are known to those not known, from what you know about the suspect or the subject to what you don't know. It's **scientific**, gathering data, completing all the information needs, bringing the interrogation "experiment" to a close.

11. **Two or More Suspects.** If there are two or more suspects, interrogate them individually briefly at first, then use one against the other to select more promising questions and better techniques for more intensive interrogation.

12. **Two or More Interrogators.** The most efficient interrogation from a cost-benefit or time study viewpoint is by one skilled interrogator. "Too many cooks spoil the broth." Disadvantages of multiple interrogators: differing personalities, conversational and questioning style and vocabulary, nonverbal behaviors, interrupted, discontinuity of relationship with the suspect, greater chance for inconsistencies, and suspects can play one interrogator against the other. More than one interrogator is a

practical necessity if there is a time squeeze or many suspects to be questioned. If a team approach is considered more practical, one person must be in charge and the interrogation should proceed with the discipline of a military mission. If there are more than two interrogators there must be a strong team spirit and open communications at regularly scheduled meetings to openly share concerns, and where brainstorming, suggestions, and criticisms considered. Two or more heads **can be** better than one, if they thoroughly know and trust each other and can work smoothly toward the common goal, much like a good marriage. If it's working, the investigation process should be improved by the team effort above and beyond what one interrogator could reasonably achieve.

13. **Multiple Sessions.** If it is necessary to continue interrogation through several sessions, it is best to end each session at some crescendo point, some anticlimax, like good theatre practice between acts and at intermission. This is an opportunity to build your case in steps and conclude a part of your work at the break time. It gives you the opportunity to recap what has been covered and so close it off in your file. You can plant seed ideas to help information flow at the next session and point to what is coming. This focusses attention in the innocent and maintains stress in the guilty. Ideally, interrogation should not be interrupted and should go "as long as it takes." More manageable for the innocent, the fatigue factor of the guilty greatly increases over time, having to lie, put up a front, worry where you're going in the questioning and what you know. Current emphasis on the rights of the accused has discouraged one continuing interrogation session.

14. **Promises, Promises.** "If I tell you will you get me off?" or words to that effect may well be the most asked question in history from suspect to interrogator. The answer should always be: "I personally can't promise you anything. . . . " It's what follows that half sentence that can become an effective interrogation technique. Certainly, it is not lawful, wise, or even possible for you to presume to speak for a prosecutor, judge, or jury. If there is a secret to expert interrogation it is to turn whatever is said and done to your advantage. In this instance, you might try: "I can't promise you anything, but if you answer these questions (or tell me all about it), I'll testify that you cooperated with this investigation and held nothing back." The sensitivity here is because to be admissible confessions must be **free** and **voluntary** and without **fear** or **favor, threat** or **promise.**

EXERCISE 38

With a coworker or in small groups if this book is used in class, role play being interrogator and suspect using a simple event as the basis for strategy and questioning, such as your last purchase in any store. Consider that purchase to be a crime. Check out your personal appearance and mannerisms. Practice reading the suspect his or her rights, evasion, lying, asking for a deal or to "cop a plea" and countering them, and the **wide net** technique from open to closed questions. Share feedback.

Problems With Admissibility and Evidence

Evidence is a legal term which means **proof** to **establish fact** at trial before a judge or jury. There are several kinds of evidence such as by eyewitness or expert witness testimony, with records and documents, or exhibits (objects). Evidence can be **direct** such as by eyewitness testimony or a videotape of a bank robbery, or **indirect** or **circumstantial** if a "chain of circumstances" which tend to confirm or deny fact. **Rules of evidence** specify **what** is admissible as evidence and the **weight** or relative importance of testimony. State and federal rules of evidence differ somewhat and you should be aware of the standards which apply to you.

Confessions are admissions of guilt for a charged offense which describe the circumstances of the offense and the suspect's part in it. Confessions are **judicial** if given in court or **extrajudicial** if given anywhere else. To be admissible as evidence, confessions must be **voluntary** which means the confessor's must be legally competent, whose mind is free of influence or coercion in the form of favor or promise, fear or threat. In most cases, confessions are **written** by hand or typed. If for any reason the suspect cannot write, you can write it for him or her but you should include the reason you are the writer. In court this could be made to look like undue influence or that you "put words in the mouth of the suspect." Confessions are: **oral** if stated and not written (spontaneous utterance), and all confessions are oral initially before being put in handwriting or typing; **implied** by silence, nodding, or indirectly if the suspect admits guilt not by open admission of guilt but by appealing to the "mercy of the court," for a lighter sentence or by a **nolo contendere** plea which neither admits nor denies charges but willing to accept fine or sentencing. **Nol pros** is when the prosecution agrees to take no further action. Confessions in the form of audio recording or videotaping are increasingly admissible in court but must be authenticated by date, time, place, and those present. A disadvantage of audiotaping, as Watergate showed, is that they can be altered.

Confessions handwritten by suspects are the easiest to defend in court since they are primary source documents in the suspect's own language and haven't been processed through a stenographer and typist. Courts and attorneys are used to typed legal documents and prefer this format which is also easier to read. Typed confessions have a disadvantage in the time lag from dictation to signing. This gives suspects a "cooling off" period to reflect and retrench into denial or flatly refuse to sign. The longer the time, the greater the chance of refusal to sign. Miranda "rights" require you to respect the suspect's right to decline signing, just as you must stop interrogation at any time the suspect opts to remain silent. Oral confessions should be witnessed by an additional person other than yourself, as an added protection in court. For the same reason, the witness should ask the subject **after** the confession: "Is that the whole truth?" The response should be noted, dated, and signed by the witnesses present.

Most confessions occur after question and answer interrogation and the confession itself can use this format. A narrative newspaper-like direct style is best and must include needed facts and details, such as the suspect's name, address, date and time of the confession, date, time, location, and circumstances (and ideally, the motive) of the crime and the suspect's part in it. Sharpen the focus if the suspect refers to the crime as "it" such as "I did it." There must be reference to the crime itself, even if in street language and not proper English or legal terminology. There should be details of what occurred before, during, and after the crime. This helps the judge or jury to visualize and understand the event. The suspect's clothes, vehicle and any objects involved, weapons or other should be included. This further confirms the suspect's identity. All of this must be in the suspect's own language and **never yours**. Poor grammar and misspelling **help** because it is further evidence the suspect, not you, wrote the confession. For this reason, some interrogators ask the suspect to state a previous address or job, social security or auto license tag numbers. VERY IMPORTANT POINT: At the confession stage of interrogation **do not speak for the suspect**. Exert careful, conscious effort **only** to help him or her focus on the facts.

Re-Mirandizing. You should recite Miranda "rights" **at the moment** the suspect states a wish to confess, and again **at time of signing** the confession. This is **in addition** to the reading of rights when the suspect is charged. Written reference to this can begin the confession, worded something like: "I have been advised I do not have to make the following statement and that it can be used against me in court. I understand I have the right to have an attorney present and that one will be provided at no cost if I cannot afford one. I waive these rights and I am making this statement voluntarily and of my own free will, without threat or promise." If you choose to do this, it might be helpful to have this preface typed beforehand so that every confessor is given the same information and can conveniently copy it verbatim into the confession.

Other important aspects of the confession phase:

1. Every page should be **initialled and dated** by the suspect, and every correction initialled and dated in the margin. If there is no marginal space, the correction should be written above the error and initialled and dated there also. If there are many or **major corrections** corrections, you should get another confession, but previous copies must be kept and may be used in court. The defense attorney may try to make it look as if you coerced, misled, or shaped the confession.

2. Oral, implied, or taped confessions should be **described and documented** in your notes, dated and signed. Oral confessions should be witnessed by .

3. Know and be prepared to describe the size and location of the interrogation room, those present, even the furniture, room temperature and lighting, to defend against defense objections of coercion or undue influence (light in the eyes, room too cold or too hot, hard chair, etc.).

4. **Read the confession aloud** to the suspect before he or she signs, to ensure it is understood and document this fact in your notes with date and time noted.

5. Hand the pen to the suspect and look down at the confession, **saying nothing**. In court, you could be accused of threatening behaviors such as "you'd better sign this if you know what's good for you" or some other lie. If you say nothing you can never be misquoted. "Sign here" may look innocent in print but can sound threatening if delivered in a loud voice with an intense stare. Hand the pen the same way you'd offer a cigarette. It's even better if your whole organization uses this nonverbal technique as standard procedure. **That** can be referred to in court if need be and is a good defense against defense insinuations and claims.

6. **Always investigate confession details** even if it appears to be an "open and shut case." In court, anything can happen. You can't overdo criminal

prosecution. Pile up the data. Take no chances. Do this even after conviction. Appeals can reopen cases and a complete file will help ensure justice in the future.

Examples of **inadmissible confessions**: defendant asks for but is not given access to an attorney, threatened with bodily harm, told to sign confession or go to prison, sign and there would be pardon, parole, or no prosecution, or not allowed to sleep, go to the bathroom, or eat until the confession is signed. Courts have held that what could "shock the conscience of a reasonable person" is sufficient grounds to declare a confession inadmissible. On the other hand, some courts have considered **confessions admissible** from the mentally ill, retarded, intoxicated, or recovering from delirium tremens (dt's) if found to have sufficient mental capacity to know what they are saying or signing and where the defendant confessed while handcuffed in custody. Evidence can be admissible obtained from an inadmissible confession! For example, if the confession included the location of the victim's body, murder weapon, stolen goods, or illegal drugs, these can be recovered and used in evidence even though the confession is ruled inadmissible. Be familiar with the rules of evidence in your local, state, and federal courts.

Entrapment is inducing someone to commit a crime not planned by that person, with the intent to prosecute. "Sting" or "scam" operations run the risk of constituting entrapment. Public officials and law enforcement officers have been cited for entrapment in cases involving prostitution, drug trafficking, and stock fraud. Section 2.13 of the *Model Penal Code* defines it as "making knowingly false representations designed to induce the belief that such conduct is not prohibited or employing methods of persuasion or inducement which create a substantial risk that such an offense will be committed by persons other than those ready to commit it" (Black, 1979).

EXERCISE 39

With coworkers or in class, discuss how you can most effectively interrogate, satisfy rules of evidence, and facilitate a confession. How far can you go before risking entrapment or an inadmissible confession? What course should you steer, rigidly according to law, loosely with maximum flexibility and deception, down the middle, veering according to the case? How will you defend your choice in court?

The Write Stuff

You can be the world's best interrogator but fail miserably if you can't take good notes. A **reporter's notebook** is a wirebound hardcover writing tablet about the size of a business envelope which fits easily into a man's inside coat pocket (left side) or a woman's purse. NEVER use loose sheets, padded paper, or 3-ring or no-ring binders. In court you can be accused of discarding notes or removing sheets. The safest notebook is one with permanently glued or sewn pages that can't be removed. But the pocket-sized reporter's notebook is best even though pages could be torn from it. Know how many pages are in a new, unused notebook and if a defense attorney ever comes at you with the insinuation you could have torn out pages, state the number of pages and suggest that any stationery store could be phoned to confirm the figure and the pages of your notebook counted by the court clerk, judge, or attorney. Don't ever tear out pages! And don't doodle on them—you may be asked in court to explain it. It's happened.

Learn to take notes efficiently. ALWAYS start notes with the date and exact time of beginning and ending of the conversation. Don't write every word—you won't be able to keep up. Take down key words and phrases. Use abbreviations but be sure you know what they mean. Include notes about any nonverbal behavior you observe ("how to" details are in Chapter 4). Carry an extra pen. Use black ink—it photocopies well.

EXERCISE 40

Take inventory of your writing materials: notebook, size, pens or pencils, where you keep and carry them, how you have been using them? Do you note nonverbal behaviors when they occur? How do your materials and how you use them compare with others? With standards in your organization? How can you and the organization improve materials and their use?

Interrogating Violent Persons

A good rule of thumb is that anyone agitated enough to be a high risk of becoming violent is too agitated to be interrogated. This is a judgment call best done on the basis of a blend of knowledge, training, and experience but with an equal dose of intuition and common sense. To paraphrase the old saying: "It ain't what you know that'll hurt you; it's what you **don't** know." Here are some common sense rules in dealing with potentially violent persons:

1. Keep the room safe, free of sharps, glass, throwable objects, and with shatterless windows. Leave your gun outside.

2. Never question anyone without backup in the immediate area, outside the room, aware you are interrogating.

3. Take control of the session from the beginning and maintain control throughout.

4. Keep cool on the outside even if you're unsure of yourself or terrified inside.

5. Watch for signs of escalating emotion, such as in the eyes, face, and mannerisms, and if there has been previous violence. If you feel at risk **ask them:** "What are you feeling right now? Do you think you may lose control? If so we can talk some other time." Be careful where you sit. Provide an unobstructed exit route out of the room for the person being interrogated. Your backup will prevent escape from the building with your help—not just you alone.

6. Anyone on drugs, prescribed or street drugs, is a risk for becoming violent. PCP, a very dangerous street drug, can produce a **toxic psychosis** and alcohol or drug withdrawal can cause extreme agitation ("the dt's").

7. Persons with certain types of mental disorders can become violent, such as: a Vietnam veteran experiencing a flashback of a combat situation (**posttraumatic stress disorder**); a **paranoid schizophrenic** acting on command hallucinations; an agitated or suicidal **depression; personality disorders** under stress; **psychopaths** or **sociopaths** who aren't getting what they want. **Delirium,** clouded, flickering consciousness, can result in restless, anxious, irritable behaviors, even paranoid delusions and hallucinations.

8. Persons having side effects of major tranquilizers (**neuroleptics**) or who have taken a drug overdose can show strange behaviors which can be misinterpreted as potentially violent. They are not. Common examples are: choking (**laryngeal-pharyngeal spasm**); tight neck muscles causing twisting the head (**dystonia**); restless movements, rapid heart rate, becoming feverish, confused or agitated (**akathisia**).

9. Know your local emergency services with clearly posted phone numbers so you don't have to look them up (hospital emergency room, rescue squad, poison center, crisis line, mental health center).

EXERCISE 41

Go over the nine points above and consider yourself in the situation described. What would you have done or have you done in the past in such situations? What can or will you do in the future?

Courtroom Survival Skills

Testifying in court can be stressful. It is as an **adversary process** and attorneys on both sides have a duty to do all in their power to present their case in the best light, to win. You can be the world's best interrogator and still be made to look like a fool in court. The fact that you speak "the truth, the whole truth, and nothing but the truth" doesn't matter when you are in the hands of an experienced trial lawyer. To further examine the influence of courtroom procedure, testimony, and "lawyering" view the movies *Inherit the Wind* with Spencer Tracy as Clarence Darrow in the Scopes "monkey" trial and *The Verdict* with Paul Newman and James Mason as opposing attorneys in a medical malpractice case.

As with all other aspects of interviewing and interrogation, the best way to cope with courtroom testimony is to **be prepared**. Know the case from beginning to end. Bring your notebook (it's OK to use it to "refresh memory"). Be prepared to be questioned about it on the witness stand. If an attorney can't get over and around your testimony, he or she is going to come after **you**. After all, that's all that's left if your testimony is airtight. You can be asked about your age, limits of experience, your judgment, methods, **anything** to cast doubt on your testimony. If it looks like an even match between defense and prosecution, the attorneys will be looking at each other's witnesses and the evidence with extreme scrutiny.

Here are some "dirty tricks" that could be used against you:

"Do you ever make mistakes?" How can you answer with anything but a "yes?" Next, the stinger: "Could you have made a mistake here?" Give a clear, factual answer and you may get a series of questions, each with a different slant and coloration, to try to get you to change the answer, to twist the truth. You may, instead, be yelled at, or whispered to sweetly, to change the wording of the reply. To use a humorous example, let's assume your final conclusion was: "The moon is made of green cheese." The **machine gun** attack might ask you if that is true for all moons everywhere, large or small, near and far, both sides or just the side facing earth, all of it or most of it. Besides the color, what **kind** of cheese is it and does **that** make a difference? You could be asked if you were ever on the moon yourself to see it first hand and confirm your conclusion. A simple fact can be turned over, under, around, and inside out in court. A simple fact can be transformed into rubber, bent and formed.

If you're young, it may be suggested you're inexperienced, if old, prejudiced and cynical, if a woman, sensitive or sentimental, if of a race other than the suspect, whatever bias goes with it. If you're a college graduate, perhaps you lack experience, common sense and wisdom; if you aren't, perhaps you're not too bright. If your voice is deep and loud you may be unsure of yourself, trying to make up for your uncertainty. If your voice is thin, it's for the same reason! Too many notes may mean you went out of your way to seek a conviction; too few notes mean you didn't care enough to do a thorough, competent job. Forget some minor detail and you may be asked "what else did you forget?" These "tricks" can cast doubt on the purest truth.

EXERCISE 42

Role play being cross-examined in court with a coworker. To be most effective, it should include every possible attack on your credibility and competence. It may hurt, but role play gives you the opportunity to feel what it might be like in court and practice coping skills. You can also get suggestions from others and feedback about your verbal and nonverbal behaviors.

Taking Care of Yourself

As we've discussed, a major change in interrogation technique over the past fifty years is increased use and success with an open, sharing conversational style. "Sympathy and understanding," Mulbar wrote, "will work where browbeating fails in nine out of ten cases" (1950, p. 6). More confessions have resulted from this method, proof beyond a doubt that it works and works well. There are two disadvantages to this method. The longer you interrogate, the more you will be exposed to these dangers which work on you like a long acting virus or a slow growing cancer.

The first danger is not managing or venting your anger. What you see and hear will sometimes be revolting, disgusting. You will hate the person who committed the crime. Untapped, unvented anger and hate are like stored up electrical charges. If they don't "blow" they'll burn you out (**burnout** is an apt word for it). You can become an overloaded nuclear reactor which gradually or suddenly goes out of control. You may try to cool down the reactor with alcohol. This might explain the too high alcoholism and suicide rate in police work. It can tear up your stomach, raise your blood pressure, make you jumpy or irritable like bare wires sparking with electricity. You can see unvented anger in the eyes, a smoldering emotional fire. If anger is overcontrolled, the eyes show the pain for a while but in time there is a cold, dead, empty look of despair. The lesson: Don't store up anger. Discharge it, safely!

The second danger is that questioning offenders can in time wear down your own values and morals. Some murderers seem like nice people! Jesus and also Socrates **were** convicted in courts of law. Washington and Jefferson were traitors to King George III, the legal authority at the time. As the years pass, you may feel more like an offender because you spend more and more time with them in close contact with **their** thoughts and feelings. Freud called doing that "swallowing the monster." In time **you become the enemy!** This may be a major contributing factor to corruption in public officials, a gradual erosion of values and standards, and the all too high suicide rate among police officers. The lesson: don't swallow the poison. Spit it out!

There is an antidote. To defend against these two dangers, center yourself in your Adult, ground yourself in your Parent, and at home, evenings and weekends, let the OK Kid out to play. Learn to side step the charging bull of anger, like a matador. Don't fight it head-on, because anger feeds on itself. It's best to develop an internal circuit breaker that shuts off the instant anger begins so that it cannot build up at all. You **can** choose not to let it happen, a form of **selective attention.** Try reminding yourself between interrogations that your function is to be a **fact-finder** and not a **feeler.** You **observe** and **gather data** as a **scientist** does, not to judge others, but as a camera with a clean lens reconstructing something that happened, a surgeon working with skill on a person he or she doesn't have to like or dislike. Talking in a **friendly** way doesn't mean there is **blind trust** between you. Finley Peter Dunne wrote in *Mr. Dooley's Philosophy* (1900) "trust everybody—**but cut the cards.**" Sometimes you won't be able to trust, and your emotions will be so strong you take them with you wherever you go. You must get it out, by talking it out with a trusted coworker on the job (so you don't take it home), jogging or working out physically, turning taped or radio music up in your car, loudly cussing out all criminals as you drive home (with windows up so nobody hears), pray, sing—even throw up if the case sickens you. Take a shower after an intensive interrogation—it's physically and mentally cleansing. Don't swallow it. Spit it out!

To prevent burnout you have to continually recharge your batteries, rededicate yourself to the value of what you're doing. Find meaning in your life, what makes you real and what makes what you do valuable. If you need help with this, check out a religious denomination, civic, service, or fraternal organization, where you can "feel good" and "do good." Life is a mission, not a career, and we are judged by what we leave behind rather than what we build or own while we're here. My mission in writing this book is not just to help you and others be better interviewers and interrogators but in some small way to leave the world a little better than I found it. What's yours?

EXERCISE 43

While this book is fresh in your mind, think about how you will use what you have learned to improve your skill. Write out your own plan of how you will do so. Share it with a coworker, preferably someone who can also write a "wish list." It will help to have a "buddy system" to keep you on schedule with your skills development and to give you feedback as to how you're doing.

WHAT YOU SHOULD HAVE LEARNED

This chapter's content builds on the material from previous chapters. It detailed the workings of the **criminal mind,** from first time offenders to **sociopaths** and **psychopaths,** the importance of finding **motive, opportunity, and means (MOM)** and as much as possible of the crime and the alleged criminal, carefully planning the overall **strategy,** selecting **tactics and techniques,** being aware of **rules of evidence** and **admissibility,** and taking nothing for granted when going to court. If you want to study legal aspects of interrogation, and more about coping in court, the following additional readings are recommended:

Black, H. C. (1979). *Black's law dictionary.* Fifth edition. St. Paul, MN: West Publishing Co. (A standard reference for legal terms and court procedures, with subjects listed alphabetically)

MacHovec, F. J. (1988). *Expert witness survival manual.* Springfield, IL: Charles C Thomas, Publisher. (Describes the theory of law, defines major ideas, and courtroom procedures with practical suggestions for coping in court and surviving intensive cross examination)

Studying actual court cases can help you avoid legal pitfalls and sharpen your interrogation skills. For state law there are seven regional *Reporters* published by West Publishing of St. Paul, Minnesota: *Atlantic* (A. 2d), *North Eastern* (N.E. 2d), *Southern* (So. 2d), *South Eastern* (S.E. 2d), *South Western* (S.W. 2d), *North Western* (N.W. 2d), and *Pacific* (P. 2d). Federal case law is reported in *Supreme Court Reporter* (S.Ct.), appeals court cases in the *Federal Reporter* (F. 2d), and U. S. District Court cases in the *Federal Supplement* (F.Supp). The abbreviations in parenthesis are used in legal citations to identify the court involved, such as: *Pierce v Georgia,* 254 S.E. 2d 838 (Georgia Supreme Court 1979). You would find that case in the 1979 *South Eastern Reporter.*

Epilog

The way to become an expert interviewer or interrogator is to develop and maintain a blend of education, training, and experience, a continuing understanding of yourself and others, and perhaps as important as all these, intuition, insight, common sense, wisdom, and judgment to put it all together. That's a tall order, I know. But isn't that what you really want to do with your life anyway? The British writer John Ruskin (1819–1900) wrote these words, especially chosen to conclude this book: "Quality is never an accident; it is always the result of intelligent effort."

APPENDIX A

REFERENCES

Aceves, J. B. & King, H. G. (1978). *Cultural anthropology.* Morristown, NJ: General Learning Press.

Allport, G. W. (1955). *Becoming: Basic considerations for a psychology of personality.* New Haven, CT: Yale University Press.

American Psychiatric Association (1987). *Diagnostic and statistical manual of mental disorders.* Third edition, revised (DSM–III–R). Washington, DC: Author.

Benedict, R. (1934). *Patterns of culture.* Boston, MA: Houghton Mifflin.

Benson, H. (1987). *Your maximum mind.* New York: Times Books.

Berne, E. (1964). *Games people play.* New York: Grove Press.

Birdwhistell, R. L. (1970). *Kinesics and context: Essays on body motion communication.* Philadelphia, PA: University of Pennsylvania Press.

Black, C. B. (1979). *Black's law dictionary.* Fifth edition. St. Paul, MN: West Publishing.

Bosmajian, H. A. (1971). *The rhetoric of nonverbal communication* Glenview, IL: Scott Foresman.

Brown, P. M. (1987). *The art of questioning: Thirty maxims of cross-examination.* New York: Macmillan.

Cleckley, H. (1941). *The mask of insanity.* St. Louis, MO: Mosby.

Conway, F. & Siegelman, J. (1978). *Snapping: America's epidemic of sudden personality change.* Philadelphia, PA: J. B. Lippincott.

Darwin, C. (1950). *The expression of the emotions in man and animals* (1873). New York: Philosophical Library.

Denton, L. (1988). Memory: Not place, but process. *APA Monitor,* November, 1988, page 4.

Drapela, V. J. (1987). *A review of personality theories.* Springfield, IL: Charles C Thomas.

Ekman, P. (1964). Body position, facial expression, and verbal behavior during interview. *Journal of Abnormal and Clinical Psychology, 68,* 295–301.

Ekman, P. (Ed.) (1982). *Emotion in the human face.* Second edition. New York: Cambridge University Press.

Ekman, P., & Friesen, W. (1972). Hand movements. *Journal of Communication, 22,* 353–374.

Ekman, P., & Friesen, W. (1975), *Unmasking the face.* Englewood Cliffs, NJ: Prentice Hall.

Ekman, P., Friesen, W., & Bear, J. (1984). The international language of gestures. *Psychology Today, 18,* 64–69.

Ekman, P., & Oster, H. (1979). Facial expressions of emotion. *Annual Review of Psychology, 30,* 527–554.

Eisenberg, A., & Smith, R. (1972). *Nonverbal communication.* New York: Bobbs Merrill.

Elliott, R. (1985). On the reliability of eyewitness testimony: A retrospective review. *Psychological Reports, 57,* 219–226.

Evans, R. I. (1970). *Gordon Allport: The man and his ideas.* New York: E. F. Dutton.

Feinberg, M. R. (October 24, 1988). When to engender fear—or at least a high degree of anxiety. New York, NY: *Wall Street Journal.*

Fensterheim, H. & Baer, J. (1975). *Don't say YES when you want to say NO.* New York: Dell.

Fisher, R. & Ury, W. (1983). *Getting to yes: Negotiating agreement without giving in.* Baltimore, MD: Penguin.

Freedman, A. M. & Kaplan, H. I. (Eds) (1971). *Interpreting personality: A survey of twentieth century views.* New York: Atheneum.

Freud, S. (1960). The psychopathology of everyday life (1901). Volume 6 of *The Standard Edition of the Complete Psychological Works of Sigmund Freud.* London, England: Hogarth Press.

Freud, S. (1953). Fragment of an analysis of a case of hysteria (1905). Volume 1 of *The Standard Edition of the Complete Psychological Works of Sigmund Freud.* London, England: Hogarth Press.

Frijda, N. H. (1988). The laws of emotion. *American, Psychologist, 43,* 349–358.

Fromm, E. (1951). *The forgotten language: An introduction to the understanding of dreams, fairy tales and myths.* New York: Rinehart.

Geiselman, R. E., & Fisher, R. P. (1985). *Interviewing victims and witnesses of crime.* Research in Brief, National Institute of Justice. Washington, DC: U. S. Department of Justice.

Glueck, S., & Glueck, E. (1950). *Unraveling juvenile delinquency.* Cambridge, MA: Harvard University Press.

Hakel, M. D. (1986). Personnel selection and placement. *Annual Review of Psychology, 37,* 351–380.

Hall, E. T. (1959). *The silent language.* New York: Doubleday.

Hall, E. T. (1963). A system of the notation of proxemic behavior. *American Anthropology, 66,* 1003–1026.

Hall, E. T. (1966). *The hidden dimension.* New York: Doubleday.

Hall, E. T. (1968). Proxemics. *Current Anthropology, 9,* 83–95.

Hammond, H. C., Hepworth, D. H. & Smith, V. G. (1977). *Improving therapeutic communication.* San Francisco, CA: Jossey-Bass.

Harris, T. (1969). *I'm OK—you're OK.* New York: Harper & Row.

Hayakawa, S. I. (1951). *Language in action.* New York: Harcourt.

Herink, R. (Ed) (1980). *The psychotherapy handbook.* New York: New American Library (Times Mirror).

Hinde, R. A. (1972) (Ed.). *Nonverbal communications.* Cambridge, England: University of Cambridge Press.

Hines, T. (1988). *Pseudoscience and the paranormal.* Buffalo, NY: Prometheus Books.

Horney, K. (1950). *Neurosis and human growth: The struggle toward self-realization.* New York: W. W. Norton.

Inbau, F. E. & Reid, J. E. (1967). *Criminal interrogation and confessions.* Baltimore, MD: Williams & Wilkins.

Karpman, B. (1961). The structure of neurosis. *Archives of Criminal Psychodynamics, 4,* 599–646.

Kelley, D. M. (1946). Preliminary studies of the Rorschach records of the Nazi war criminals. *Rorschach Research Exchange, 10,* 45–48.

Knapp, M. L. (1972). *Nonverbal communication in human interaction.* New York: Holt Rinehart.

Leeds, D. (1987). *Smart questions.* New York, NY: McGraw-Hill.

Levin, E. (1980). *Levin's laws: Tactics for winning without intimidation.* New York: M. Evans.

Loftus, E. F. (1979). *Eyewitness testimony.* Cambridge, MA: Harvard University Press.

Loftus, E. (1983). Whose shadow is crooked? *American Psychologist, 38,* 576–577.

MacHovec, F. J. (1973). *Freud: His contributions to modern thought.* White Plains, NY: Peter Pauper Press.

MacHovec, F. J. (1974). *Awareness and sensitivity: Exercises and techniques.* White Plains, NY: Peter Pauper Press.

MacHovec, F. J. (1974). *Games we all play—and shouldn't.* White Plains, NY: Peter Pauper Press.

MacHovec, F. J. (1974). *So you think you're crazy? Reassurance concerning everyday hangups.* White Plains, NY: Peter Pauper Press.

MacHovec, F. J. (1975). *Body talk: A handbook on nonverbal behavior.* White Plains, NY: Peter Pauper Press.

MacHovec, F. J. (1978). The evil eye: Superstition or hypnotic phenomenon? *American Journal of Clinical Hypnosis, 19,* 74–79.

MacHovec, F. J. (1986). *Hypnosis complications: Prevention and risk management.* Springfield, IL: Charles C Thomas.

MacHovec, F. J. (1987). *Expert witness survival manual.* Springfield, IL: Charles C Thomas.

MacKinnon, R. A. & Michels, R. (1971). *The psychiatric interview in clinical practice.* Philadelphia, PA: W. B. Saunders.

Makay, J. & Gaw, B. A. (1975): *Personal and interpersonal communication: Dialogue with the self and others.* Columbus, OH: Charles E. Merrill.

Maslow, A. H. (1968). *Toward a psychology of being.* Second edition. New York: Van Nostrand. Reinhold.

Maslow, A. H. (1969). *The psychology of science: A reconnaisance.* Chicago, IL: Henry Regnery.

Maslow, A. H. (1970). *Motivation and personality.* Second edition. New York: Harper & Row.

Maslow, A. H. (1971). *The farther reaches of human nature.* New York: Viking Press.

McCoid, J. C. (1974). *Civil procedure: Cases and materials.* St. Paul, MN: West Publishing.

McKay, M., Davis, M. & Fanning, P. (1983). *Messages: The communication book.* Oakland, CA: New Harbinger.

McLaughlin, J. M. (1977). *Practical trial evidence.* New York, NY: Practicing Law Institute.

Mead, M. (1975). Review of Darwin and facial expression. *Journal of Communications, 25,* 209–213.

Meerloo, J. A. M. (1949). *Delusion and mass delusion.* New York: Nervous and Mental Disease Monographs.

Meerloo, J. A. M. (1956). *The rape of the mind: The psychology of thought control, menticide, and brainwashing.* New York: World Publishing.

Mehrabian, A. (1972). *Nonverbal communication.* Chicago, IL: Aldine Atherton.

Miller, G. A. (1973). *Communication language and meaning.* New York: Basic Books.

Morrison, M. W. (1988). Psychological assessment of eyewitness testimony. *American Journal of Forensic Psychology, 6,* 37–48.

Mulbar, H. (1951). *Interrogation.* Springfield, IL: Charles C Thomas.

Nirenberg, J. S. (1963). *Getting through to people.* Englewood Cliffs, NJ: Prentice-Hall.

Offer, D. & Sabshin, M. (1974). *Normality: Theoretical and clinical concepts of mental health.* New York: Basic Books.

Packard, V. (1957). *The hidden persuaders.* New York: David McKay.

Peck, M. S. (1981). *People of the lie.* New York: Simon and Schuster.

Platonov, K. I. (1959). *The word as a physiological and therapeutic factor.* Moscow, USSR: Foreign Languages Publishing House.

Prichard, J. C. (1837). *A treatise on insanity and other disorders affecting the minor.* Philadelphia, PA: Howell, Barington and Haswell.

Raimo, A. M. (1987). Psychological challenges to eyewitness testimony. *American Journal of Forensic Psychology, 5,* 23–36.

Reader's Digest Association (1964). *Secrets and spies: Behind the scenes stories of World War II.* Pleasantville, NY: Author.

Reich, W. (1949). *Character analysis.* New York: Orgone Press.

Resorta, R. A. (1988). Pavlovian conditioning: It's not what you think it is. *American Psychologist, 43,* 151–160.

Ritzler, B. A. (1978). The Nuremberg mind revisited: A quantitative approach to Nazi Rorschach. *Journal of Personality Assessment, 47,* 344–353.

Rosen, R. D. (1977). *Psychobabble.* New York: Avon Books.

Ruesch, J. (1973). *Therapeutic communication.* New York: W. W. Norton.

Salama, A. A. (1988). The antisocial personality (the sociopathic personality). *Psychiatric Journal of the University of Ottawa, 13,* 149–153.

Sapir, E. A. (1958). *Culture, language, and personality.* Berkeley, CA: University of California Press.

Sargant, W. E. (1957). *Battle for the mind.* New York: Doubleday.

Scheflen, A. E. (1963). The significance of posture in communication systems. *Psychiatry, 27,* 316–331.

Shostrom, E. L. (1967). *Man, the manipulator.* New York: Abingdon Press.

Simon, R. I. (1988). *Concise guide to clinical psychiatry and the law.* Washington, DC: American Psychiatric Press.

Smith, S. (1979). Remembering in and out of context. *Journal of Experimental Psychology, 5,* 460–471.

Steiner, C. (1974). *Scripts people live.* New York: Grove Press.

Stewart, I., & Joines, V. (1987). *TA today: A new introduction to transactional analysis.* Chapel Hill, NC: Lifespace Publishing.

Stuller, J. (1984). Winning by negotiation. *Kiwanis magazine,* October, pp. 18, 19, 48.

Sullivan, H. S. (1954). *The psychiatric interview.* New York: W. W. Norton.

Tannen, D. (1986). *That's not what I meant: How conversational style makes or breaks your relations with others.* New York: William Morrow.

Thayer, S. (1988). Close encounters. *Psychology Today, 22,* 30–36.

Trager, G. L. (1958). Paralanguage: A first approximation. *Studies in Linguistics, 13,* 1–12.

Tulving, E. (1985). How many memory systems are there? *American Psychologist, 40,* 385–398.

Vaillant, G. E. (1986). *Empirical studies of ego mechanisms of defense.* Washington, DC: American Psychiatric Association.

Vygotsky, L. S. (1962). *Thought and language.* New York: Wiley.

Waldinger, R. J. (1984). *Psychiatry for medical students.* Washington, DC: American Psychiatric Press, Inc.

Weiner, M., Devow, S., Rubinow, S., & Geller, J. (1972). Monverbal behavior and nonverbal communication. *Psychological Review, 79,* 185–214.

Weiner, M., & Mehrabian, A. (1958). *Language within language: Immediacy, a channel in verbal communication.* New York: Appleton-Century-Crofts.

Zedeck, S., & Cascio, W. F. (1984). Psychological issues in personnel decisions. *Annual Review of Psychology, 35,* 461–518.

Zeligs, M. A. (1957). The psychology of silence: Its role in transference, countertransference, and the psychoanalytic process. *Journal of the American Psychoanalytic Association 9,* 7–43.

Zillmer, E., Archer, R. P., & Castino, R. (1989). Rorschach responses of Nazi war criminals: A reanalysis using current scoring and interpretation practices. *Journal of Personality Assessment, 53,* 85–99.

INDEX

Interview and Interrogation